Yonderings

Yonderings
Trails and Memories of the Big Bend

BEN H. ENGLISH

TCU
Press

Fort Worth, Texas

Copyright © 2017 by Ben H. English

Library of Congress Cataloging-in-Publication Data

Names: English, Ben H., author.
Title: Yonderings : trails and memories of the Big Bend / Ben H. English.
Description: Fort Worth, Texas : TCU Press, [2017]
Identifiers: LCCN 2017017778 (print) I LCCN 2017021624 (ebook) I
    ISBN 9780875656816 I ISBN 9780875656687?(alk. paper)
Subjects: LCSH: English, Ben H.--Homes and haunts--Texas--Big Bend
    Region. I
    English, Ben H.--Childhood and youth. I English, Ben
    H.--Travel--Texas--Big Bend Region. I Big Bend Region (Tex.)
    --Description
    and travel. I Big Bend Region (Tex.)--Social life and customs.
    Classification: LCC F392.B54 (ebook) I LCC F392.B54 E55 2017 (print) I
    DDC 976.4/93--dc23
LC record available at https://urldefense.proofpoint.com/v2/url?u=https-
3A__lccn.loc.gov_2017017778&d=DwIFAg&c=7Q-FWLBTAxn3T_E3
HWrzGYJrC4RvUoWDrzTlitGRH_A&r=O2eiy819IcwTGuw-
vrBGiVdmhQxMh2yxeggw9qlTUDE&m=n_70bkSKr4mIyFu3eiC
3YKXZ6vzOSwZlbLcWvxFvB1c&s=AV-3D4NVvy59FUHXdf2Bz-
lZonqaGJmbjd5IzMpwOpLA&e=

TCU Press
TCU Box 298300
Fort Worth, Texas 76129
817.257.7822
www.prs.tcu.edu
To order books: 1.800.826.8911

Designed by Bill Brammer
www.fusion29.com
Cover illustration by Ethan L'Amour English

Unless otherwise noted, all photos are from the English family collection.

*To those who came before, and to my beloved wife
who has listened to me tell their stories.*

CONTENTS

FOREWORD

The Big Bend is the most isolated, most recently settled, and most sparsely populated part of Texas. Ranchers did not arrive there with herds of cattle until the 1880s and, because it takes one hundred acres or so to support one cow and her calf, they remain few and far between. The country is so poor that, as my rancher friend Ted Gray of Alpine used to say, "Everyone who lives down there has had to do something wrong once in their life just to get by." The tiny community of Lajitas, which lies on the north bank of the Rio Grande in the heart of the Big Bend, was founded in 1901 by H.W. McGuirk, who opened a store and saloon there to cater to the mercury miners at the nearby Terlingua mines. Sixty years later the mines were closed but the store was still there, catering largely to customers from Mexico who forded the river to buy groceries and sell smuggled candelilla wax, which commanded a higher price in the United States than it did across the river in Mexico. Ben English's grandfather ran that store, which, except for the addition of a soft drink machine, was pretty much like it was when H.W. McGuirk opened it. The surrounding country had not changed much since McGuirk's time, either.

Ben English was two years old when his grandfather took over the Lajitas store in 1961, and he spent the weekends and summers of his growing-up years hanging around the store and exploring the trails that crisscross the Big Bend, many of which are now hiking paths in Big Bend National Park and Big Bend Ranch State Park. Like many people who grew up in the Big Bend fifty years ago, English is a nineteenth-century Texan living in the twenty-first century. He values his self-reliance, his outdoor skills, and his ability to take care of himself, his wife, and his two boys. He is a former Marine and a retired peace officer with a gentle, self-deprecating demeanor that tells you louder than any words not to get crosswise with him. This book is about his love of the country he grew up in.

English's career took him away from the Big Bend, first into the Marines, then to college and marriage in San Angelo, and then to the Department of Public Safety in Ozona, but he and his family spent many weekends and every vacation hiking and backpacking in the Big Bend, an activity to which he attributes the fact that his two sons became the first two graduates of Ozona High School to graduate from the United States Naval Academy at Annapolis.

English describes these hikes with an eye for the terrain that only a seasoned outdoorsman has, mixing his accounts with stories about things that happened along the Big Bend's trails long before his time, stories he absorbed from the old-timers who hung around the Lajitas store in his youth. His technique is similar to that employed by John Graves in *Goodbye to a River*, a mixture of history and natural history, and it has the same effect on the reader, rendering the landscape timeless in relation to the short time that humans have occupied it.

Ben English is the same breed as some of the men and women raised in the Big Bend that I have written about: Bill Dodson, who started making candelilla wax when he was six because his mother had married a sixteen-year old *vaquero* and who told me that he was the only Anglo who ever made wax in the Big Bend, adding, "and I didn't volunteer" ; Mojella Moore, whose mother once told her it wasn't that they were too poor to go to town, they just didn't have any money; and Wilborn Elliott, who left home at fourteen and hitchhiked from Johnson Ranch to Espanola, New Mexico, to attend McCurdy Mission School. They are a breed with a powerful respect for the landscape of the Big Bend, because they understand its perils and dangers, and they stand in sharp contrast to the urbanites who tear through it on dirt bikes or observe it through the windows of an air-conditioned RV. English recounts encounters with both of these types.

Ben English is a literary descendent of J.O. Langford, who came to the Big Bend in 1909 and wrote a fine book about it called *A Homesteader's Story*, in which he described the beautifully flowering pitahaya cactus, the tornillo bushes, the doves, the wailing of the coyotes at night, the sound of the river, and the play of light in the afternoon on the Sierra del Carmen. Since Langford's time a number of writers have tried to capture the atmosphere of this unique, spacious, and sparsely beautiful part of Texas. Most of them have not succeeded. With the publication of *Yonderings*, English joins a select group of men and women, not more than a half dozen, who have.

LONN TAYLOR
Fort Davis, Texas

Acknowledgments

— Cathy English, wife and critic, proofreader,
computer whiz, soulmate

— Captain Benjamin Levi English, USMC,
elder son and continuing partner-in-crime

— Lieutenant Ethan L'Amour English, USN,
younger son and also continuing partner-in-crime.
Thanks for the book cover, Mijo!

— Rosa Lynn English, mother and motivator who
wanted me to be something respectable like a doctor
or a lawyer. Sorry, Mom; this is as good as it gets.

— Margaret English Garrett, surviving aunt
and zealous curator of the family records.

— To TCU Press, who gambled on an unpublished author,
and to its staff who so graciously and patiently guided me
through the maze of making a thought into a reality.

. . . and to my other family and friends at large,
who have not only shared their memories
but also their lives with me. They were, and are,
true Texans one and all.

The farther backward you can look,
the farther forward you are likely to see.

—WINSTON CHURCHILL

I was two years old when we settled in the Big Bend. My grandfather, Edward Benton 'Bennie' English Jr., moved from South Texas to Lajitas in 1961. Yet members of my family on both sides had lived in this area since before the turn of the past century. The first of these was Lucinda English Hay, the eldest daughter of Captain Levi English, noted Indian fighter, pioneer, and ranger, who came to Texas in the 1820s. He was my great-great-great-great-grandfather, and my oldest son carries the same name.

Lucinda, known in the family as "Sis," was married to Silas Hay in 1859. Silas was the son of John Silas Hay Sr., another well-known ranger and pioneer who, along with Captain Levi, helped found and settle the Carrizo Springs area. When Marfa was little more than a raw railroad stop, Lucinda and Silas moved their family from Carrizo Springs by wagon and became well-regarded citizens of the growing community. She passed away in 1919 and is buried in the Marfa cemetery, along with other members of her immediate family.

Three years earlier another relative of mine came to the Big Bend. He was my grandfather on my mother's side, Private Howell Coatis Cash, United States Army. A young man in search of adventure, he enlisted just before the Glenn Spring raid by Villistas in May of 1916. His was one of the outfits rushed to the border, and he was actually stationed in Lajitas for some time before the Army discovered that Private Cash was only sixteen years old. He was thanked for his enthusiasm to serve his country and

Plaque Honoring Levi English, Early Texas Pioneer,
at Courthouse in Carrizo Springs, Texas

sent home to his grandparents in Winters. A personal treasure of
mine is his Mexican Border Service pin.

The next member of my family to make her mark in this area
was someone who still possesses a certain amount of local notoriety. Margaret English Smith was my Grandfather English's
aunt, and she ran the Langford Hot Springs site for many years
until forced out by the National Park Service. My father, Edward
Benton "Ben" English III, used to tell me that when he was a kid
the closest his family came to taking a vacation was when visiting
Aunt Mag in the Big Bend. My grandfather would load up their
car with camping supplies, a tent, and whatever other provisions
he deemed necessary and head west at every chance offered.

A tough, formidable woman in most every conceivable way,
Maggie Smith was a legend on both sides of the river because of
her many escapades as a store merchant, trader, midwife, make-
do medic, circumstantial philanthropist, and unrepentant smuggler of candelilla wax. Most people knew her simply as Maggie
or Aunt Mag, as she was called by family and her many friends.
Though Aunt Mag has been gone for several decades now, folks

Howell Coatis Cash, Private, United States Army

continue to be enthralled by her and repeat the stories of her life on the river. She was one of those larger-than-life characters that God created to match this larger-than-life country.

It was Aunt Mag who helped make it possible for my Grandfather English to obtain a lease on the Lajitas Trading Post. That old store has been there for nearly as long as Lajitas has been in existence, and continues to stand as a timeworn reminder of days long past. As far as I know my grandfather had never run a store before in his life, but he dearly wanted to plant some roots in the Big Bend. A man's man among men, he had already done a great many other things in his time. A sixth generation Texan, 'Papa' had been a cowboy, peace officer, tick force rider, ranch foreman, game warden, and truck driver, and had served two terms as sheriff in Zavala County, Texas.

Through it all he managed to raise two children, stay married to the same woman, and earn a reputation as a tough, no-nonsense sort of man who asked no quarter from this world or much of anything else. Barrel-chested and of medium height with hard,

Sheriff Edward Benton 'Ben' English Jr.,
Zavala County, Texas, in 1954

knowing eyes which peered out from under the brim of a well-worn felt Stetson, he seldom smiled except in the company of his closest friends or when playing with his grandkids. It would be currently popular to refer to him as "old school" but that doesn't near cover his essential nature; one would be more accurate in saying that he not only built that school but had gone from being its youngest pupil to the headmaster himself. If I had one role model growing up and someone whom I remained in utter awe of, it was my Papa English.

Soon after my grandparents moved to Lajitas, my mom and dad followed suit. The trading post had living quarters attached to it, as was customary for the era in which it was constructed. We lived there together until my dad went to work for Casner Motors of Alpine. But there were still frequent trips to Lajitas to help manage the trading post, our ranching interests, and the candelilla wax business. As I had not started school yet, much of that time was spent living with my grandparents.

Aunt Mag was also the person who showed my grandfather how the candelilla business worked. She had been a buyer for decades while at the Hot Springs and passed much of her knowledge on to him. *Candelilla* is a native plant which grows in this part of Texas as well as many sections of northern Mexico. Also known as *yerba*, it was utilized in various consumer products such as cosmetics, varnish, chewing gum, phonograph records, and polishing compounds, among other items. When other waxes became scarce or unavailable during wartime, candelilla was pressed into service for sundry military purposes, including the waterproofing of supplies.

As the demand for candelilla outstripped the supply in the Trans Pecos sections of Texas, the wax traders looked south to the vast numbers of the plants found in the Chihuahuan Desert of Mexico. But therein lay a problem, as candelilla was deemed a nationalized natural resource by their government. It could be legally shipped out of Mexico, but the attending restrictions and tariffs were considered excessive by many of the Mexican producers. So the base form of the wax, called *cerote*, was smuggled out, and many of the prime routes arrowed across the river and into the Big Bend. Along with his automobile dealerships, Mr. Casner was also commonly acknowledged as the biggest candelilla buyer in that part of Texas. The wax we purchased was sold to him, and he in turn further refined it for large shipments back east.

Not too long after going to work for Mr. Casner, my dad was offered the opportunity to manage Casner Motors of Presidio. My parents had only just moved to Marfa, yet they packed up again for this border town, known as one of the earliest pioneer settlements in the American Southwest. In the fall of 1963, I began my formal education on the front row of Mrs. Franco's first grade classroom. I remember being quite excited to learn that the school mascot was a blue devil, and I went home that very afternoon to exclaim to my mom that her oldest son was "a little blue devil" now. From that day forward my mom has frequently commented that I have been a little blue devil ever since.

Yet the best part of this particular move was that Presidio only sat about fifty miles upriver from Lajitas. Furthermore, the same year my grandparents took over the trading post a new highway was completed between these two points and christened Texas

FM 170. It is more commonly called by two other names given by those whom it helped most: the River Road, or *El Camino del Rio*. This paved two-lane changed daily life for many people living along that stretch of the Rio Grande, making it far easier to get back and forth through the imposing terrain. As this route has become better known, it has gained a deserved reputation as being one of the most visually dramatic drives found anywhere in the United States.

The River Road also proved to be of major benefit to me personally, as it provided ready access to spend ample time with my grandparents. During those years a bus service ran between the two locales; though their "fleet" actually consisted of only one vehicle, a 1959 Chevy station wagon as black as a moonless night and with no air-conditioning. Even after starting school in Presidio I was usually headed for Lajitas most every weekend, in addition to school breaks and throughout the long, hot summers. My family was probably as responsible as anyone else in keeping that little bus line solvent, because I rode it a lot of miles and can remember frequently being the only passenger aboard.

At the far end of every round-trip was a young boy's heaven on earth. I had boots, a cowboy hat, a jenny to ride, and most importantly, pretty much the run of the place. My grandfather not only had holdings around Lajitas but also in the surrounding area running from Fresno Canyon to north of the Agua Fria, down the far side of Terlingua Creek, and back again. Where he went, often enough so did I. Thus began a lifelong education and budding love affair with the tens of thousands of square miles of Big Bend country beyond that tiny dot on the map marked *Lajitas*.

My grandfather was an exacting man in many ways but with a soft spot for children, especially grandchildren, and in a womanly way the same could be said of my grandmother. My frequent stays with them allowed the juices of boyhood to flow freely, and they indulged me as only grandparents can their oldest grandchild. But above all they gave me freedom, freedom to go and do as few children my age could ever begin to imagine. It gave vent to the insatiable desire to know what lies around the next bend in the canyon or over the far hill. Born of a family with the innate urge to go and see beyond what the eye could first perceive, for me the die was cast at conception and it came as natural as breathing. Perhaps in some ways, it was just as essential. Of all

Lyndon and Ben H. English, Fulcher Place, 1967

the wonderful gifts and unconditional love they ever gave me, that freedom was the most precious of all.

A few years later my father decided to join my grandfather full-time in their shared ranching/general store/candelilla wax venture, and together they bought the old Fulcher Ranch. Divided down the middle by the broad banks of Terlingua Creek, its origins went back to when much of the place was known as the Reed Ranch. Al Reed, who was patriarch of that clan, was a storekeeper and mine owner of some local repute as well as being a rancher. In a dispute over a wagon sold on credit, he was killed in a gun battle early in May of 1899. Reed Plateau is named after him, as was the old Al Reed Trail, which ran north from near the Colquitt-Tigner Mine. Another area landmark linked to the name was a set of rock corrals near our ranch headquarters, said to have been originally constructed by the Reed family. I expended a lot of sweat and effort helping repair those corrals during the time we had the place.

Sometime later the Fulchers came along and made the Reed place and other portions of the surrounding land their own. Daisy Fulcher, who was our local postmaster, entertained my family on many occasions with stories of the Big Bend and the people who had lived there. A somewhat snaggletoothed woman of middle age with a constant twinkle in her eyes from behind

Barry, Ben H., Edward Benton 'Ben' III, and Lyndon English, 1968

large framed glasses, Daisy loved to give hugs and kisses to the unwary or slow-footed, whether they liked it or not. She also had a heart of gold, and would cackle with glee at a good joke or just because she felt like it. Like those she so often spoke of, Daisy was another one of the unforgettable folks you meet in a country that readily produces such a unique breed.

My dad was a strict disciplinarian and no more so than with his oldest son, whom he sometimes referred to as "The Prototype." At the age of ten years I was expected to do a man's work in the saddle and woe unto me if any assignment was not faithfully carried out. Then there were the chores; when you lived on a ranch with no electricity, no telephone, and no outside entertainment, there always seemed to be plenty of chores to keep one occupied. We broke horses, rounded up cattle, hauled water, built dikes, improved primitive roads, repaired water gaps, and did a hundred other things involving hard work that never seemed to cease. Only later did I realize that while my grandparents had given me freedom, my dad provided equal amounts of responsibility and instilled in me a strong streak of independence. Both are two of the principal foundations for becoming what every boy desires most: to be called a man.

There was also school, a public education system referred to as the Terlingua School District. It was a single classroom affair

Terlingua School, 1967 (author in foreground)

for six grades, divided from a like room used as a combination library/storage space by a breezeway in the middle. To one side sat a small travel trailer for use by the school's only teacher. The facilities were minimal at best: open windows for warm weather, a single gas heater for cold, and outhouses for when the need arose. As best I can recall there was a total of nine students usually, and somehow my dad ended up as president of the school board. Knowledge was important to him, whether I wanted to be a willing recipient or not.

Like many other puzzles in the Big Bend, Terlingua School was actually located on the outskirts of Study Butte. My mom, Rosa Lynn English, drove a baby-blue '63 Ford Galaxie 500 sedan about fifty miles a day round-trip just to get us there and back. This was mostly along a lonely, isolated track known as South County Road, which had started out as a wagon trail during the cinnabar boom of the 1890s. Before the early 1950s, the battered route had been part of the main thruway between Terlingua and Alpine. My mom only knew one way to drive it, too, and that was wide open with clouds of dust boiling behind like a Phantom jet on afterburner. I think she believed that if she drove it fast enough that rock strewn, rutted, rubbing board-surfaced grade would somehow smooth itself out. Strangely enough, the body of that old Ford was as solid the day she traded it in as when it

Lynn, Ben H., Lyndon, Barry, and Regina English,
The Rockpile in Fort Davis Mountains

left the factory. I cannot say the same for the suspension.

My younger brother Lyndon and I were about the only Anglos who attended the school during those years. That was another education of an entirely different sort, and one that made my own life and outlook so much richer in content. I busted the piñata far more times than I ever pinned the tail on the donkey, and we often distressed our mother when she learned of our trading her handmade-with-love sandwiches for equally handmade-with-love tortillas and frijoles. English was the only language accepted while inside the confines of the schoolhouse, but the Spanish tongue permeated most everyplace else when among our peers and their families. Those friends who knew me after we moved to Fort Stockton still kid about me speaking English with a south-of-the-border accent.

Yes the day did come when we moved once again to a more "civilized" part of Texas. There were valid reasons given for the change: the candelilla demand was down, the cattle market was akin to playing Russian roulette with only one empty chamber, and my parents felt we were not getting a proper formal education. There were also more private family matters that needed to be addressed. But to a twelve-year-old boy, no reason merited leaving a place he loved so much; I can still remember crying

Ben H. English, USMC, 1976

upon hearing the news. Fort Stockton might have only been about 175 miles away, but in my young mind it might as well have been on the moon and designated by a large sign that spelled out *H-E-L-L*.

A saving grace was that my grandparents remained in the Big Bend for a few more years, though no longer at the trading post. When we would go see them I could not help but notice how the land was changing. There were more people, more roads, more power poles, more telephones, and even television, thanks to a repeater tower placed on Willow Mountain. The many technological advances of the late twentieth century were finally getting the upper hand on this wistful, lonely land.

My dad continued to try to ranch via long distance, driving down to the Big Bend every weekend he could, and I went along when possible. However, that parting stratagem soon played out with far too predictable results. We were out of the Big Bend for good, but there wasn't much good to be found in that depressing reality. Not long afterwards, Dad left Mom, and she was now alone with four kids to raise. After that happened there wasn't much time for going to the Big Bend or anyplace else; my years in high school were a jumbled blur of menial jobs, growing pains, and hard times in general.

I enlisted in the Marine Corps at seventeen and spent the next

Ben H. English, THP, 2001

seven years feeding that same restless need to go and see. During that time I also managed to make myself into a half-decent Marine, mentored along by some of the finest examples of men I have ever known. After my second hitch I pulled the pin, came back to Texas, and attended college at Angelo State. There I obtained a degree, got married, and managed to be accepted to the All Service Recruit Academy for the Texas Department of Public Safety. My first and only duty station was Highway Patrol Area 4B7-Ozona, where by the Grace of God I spent my entire career and was able to retire still healthy and near the top of my game.

All the while the siren song of the Big Bend continued to sound in my head. I came near to going to Sul Ross State rather than ASU, but there were more opportunities for me in San Angelo concerning what I had planned for my future. Make that *our* future, because ASU is where I met the only woman who actually understood me and didn't demand some sort of change from what I was inside. Of course, after the wedding our shoe-string financed honeymoon involved going to the Big Bend. That was only the first of many trips we shared together, and Cathy caught the bug, too.

Both of us wanted to live there. However, there were no openings to be had in any of the highway patrol stations within that

Cathy, Rachel, Levi, Ben H,, and Ethan English, 2015

area. The troopers in those substations were older men committed to their families and the communities they served, and flamethrowers and machine gun fire couldn't flush them out. By the time those slots became available for a younger officer such as myself, Cathy and I had already established our family in Ozona, and our sons had started school.

Nevertheless, this didn't mean we just forgot about the idea. In the decades that followed, our two sons became accomplished young men. They were valedictorians of their respective high school classes, UIL state champs in both academics and athletics, Eagle Scouts, and the first two students from Ozona High School to graduate from the United States Naval Academy at Annapolis. I mention this only because a very real part of who they turned out to be is unalterably linked to our numerous trips camping out and backpacking in the Big Bend. You young parents out there take note: your child's most important star to steer by is you, and what you teach them is most likely what they will in turn become.

The following pages are commentaries concerning a few of

those trips and the lessons learned along the way, as well as a written document containing some of the personal knowledge gained of this land. But no matter how much knowledge I have accumulated, it will never equal the accompanying curiosity I possess about the Big Bend. There will always be more questions than answers, and perhaps that is as it should be.

It is a land that excites the imagination, and it is part of human nature to depict fanciful things and events which never really happened that way, or never even happened at all. I have attempted to stay as true and factual as possible in what I have written; that facet of my work is very important to me. If I wasn't sure of the facts, I said as much or left the story to those who entertain the sympathetic passerby with fanciful repertoire of personal tall tales. Who knows? One or two of them might actually be true.

I do hope you enjoy this book. More so, I hope that you are able to travel some of these same trails, which carry so many good memories for me. If life is a highway, those paths have proven to be the scenic routes to very special places most folks seldom see or experience. Finally, it is my sincerest hope that you find them filled with as much happiness and fulfillment as I have over the past fifty years and more.

Cuidado y vaya con Dios,
Ben H. English
Ozona, Texas

CHAPTER 1

The Perfect Place
for a Pterodactyl Farm

*It is easier to build strong children
than to repair broken men.*

—FREDERICK DOUGLASS

"Here they come," she would say, standing on the front porch of the old Lajitas Trading Post. Even after all these years I can still see her in my mind: left hand cupped over her forehead as she peered southward with dark, intense eyes. The desert breeze played with the stray strands of gray hair which had escaped her bobby pins. A somewhat petite middle-aged woman who came from Irish and Cherokee kin, my grandmother was as tough and resilient as the roughhewn high ground she now surveyed.

"Where?" I asked excitedly, my own eyes following hers towards the forbidding-looking uplift which filled most of the southern horizon.

"Up there," she said, pointing with her right index finger for emphasis. "They're just starting through the saddle on the mesa."

I remained silent, searching vainly along where the trail came through the pass for any sign of what she was talking about.

"Don't you see them, son?" she asked, the slightest hint of exasperation in her voice.

"No, Granny," I answered in a hesitating fashion, still looking hard and seeing nothing.

"You need your mom and dad to get your eyesight checked, Bennie Howell."

"Yes ma'am," I would respond dejectedly.

Heading out for the saddle atop Anguila Mesa

Some members of our family only used my full name when I was in trouble; usually deep trouble. But with her it was a term of endearment. Or perhaps because she had a husband, a son, and a father-in-law all with the first name of Ben, she felt the need for some differentiation in the name of her eldest grandson. Whatever the case, for me it was always Bennie Howell or *Benito*.

"Well, I suppose we had best start making ready for them," she would announce, running her hand back over the top of her head in an attempt to smooth down those errant strands of hair. "Your Papa will be in from the Madrid after a while and he'll need supper before they get here." She would walk through the large open doorway of the store before making her way to our adjacent living quarters.

"You keep an eye on things," she'd call out over her shoulder. "I'll be back in the kitchen."

"Yes ma'am."

I'd keep my seat, looking furtively for that incoming candelilla wax load until she either called me in for something or I managed to finally spot them trudging toward Lajitas. Years later I found out that I did need glasses, but even with them on I was never able to see as well as that old woman could at distance. Until her very last days she had the eyesight of a white-tailed hawk.

Hours later, often after the sun had gone down, the plodding train of burros and men would move quietly into the trading post area. Heavily loaded with tow sacks bulging with the tannish-colored chunks of wax along with the white plastic bleach bottles in which the men carried their water, the little animals plodded along, eyes half closed as if falling asleep or perhaps dreaming of someplace cool with no more loads to carry. Every once in awhile, they would flick their long ears or swish their tails in annoyance at the insects which seemed to follow them about.

Hot, tired, and dirty, the men and their animals would come to a halt near the weight scales on the west side of the store, and our part in their arduous journey would begin. The tow sacks of semi-processed candelilla, usually weighing in the neighborhood of fifty to sixty pounds, would be offloaded from the burros, dumped out for a cursory examination, and then placed on the heavy iron platform scales. A tally sheet was kept and agreed to by both seller and buyer.

Once finished, the men would be paid in American dollars or have the money put on account to pick up the necessities they needed, along with an occasional luxury from inside the store. The trading post was exactly that: a place where one could buy or barter for food, clothing, personal items, household needs, hats, boots, belts, beer, candy, provisions, tools, ammunition, and a hundred other different things. It was the last of its kind in this country; some claim the establishment was built as early as 1899, while others set the year at 1915.

Whatever the exact date, it made for a profitable business under the ownership of Lajitas founder and first citizen H. W. McGuirk. In the decades to come the trading post would change hands numerous times. Throughout it all it served not only as a source of provisions but as a community meeting spot for area locals on both sides of the river. By the 1960s, it was an enduring relic symbolizing a way of life which was vanishing in this remote border area.

English was hardly ever spoken; the language of choice for conducting business was Mexican Spanish, and both of my grandparents were fluent. Soft strains of conversations along with occasional laughter would mix with the *canciones del norteño* emanating from the jukebox on the front porch. After securing their needs the men would congregate in that area, sitting in wooden booths or on the raised platform itself. There they would talk among themselves, some drinking Lone Stars and Falstaffs while others sipped on soda pops and listened to the music. This would last into the wee hours of the next morning, or even beyond. For them it was the briefest of breaks from a bitterly hard, backbreaking, and sometimes dangerous existence.

When the time came they and their burros would reverse direction and head back to Mexico, sometimes skirting the river side of the mesa and sometimes climbing directly over the top whence they came. The line of men and burros would grow smaller and smaller as they made their way up the steep trail until becoming one with the unforgiving desert which they knew so well.

There are a lot of rugged and desolate places in the Big Bend of Texas, but Anguila Mesa would make the short list of most anyone who knows something of this hard, sun-seared land. For me as a child it was a fabled place to while away hours of speculation, as are most places where a young boy is forbidden to go. Even at five years old I mostly had the run of the nearby area, often riding on the back of an aged jenny called Becky. I could ride anywhere other than over the highway, across the river, or toward Anguila Mesa; especially toward the mesa. In fact, I was forbidden to go even as far as our hay fields, which lay between it and Lajitas.

I never violated those boundaries, mostly due to the great respect and outright fear I had of my grandfather. He was the second Ben and about as tough a customer as you would likely run into on either side of the Rio Grande. Cowboy, rancher, sheriff, river rider, and all around hombre, his word was law, or as close as you could get to law in Lajitas, Texas, circa 1963. I still vividly remember the one time I didn't do as he had said and got a nylon rope across my behind for the trouble. I may be slow in a lot of ways, but he made me a true believer early on.

And as usual he had good reason. Lajitas was about as far away from anyplace else and as close to the end of the earth as you could find in the Lone Star State during that era. In many ways, it was like stepping back into the nineteenth century compared to what most other children of my generation ever experienced. Looking back I now realize that was probably why I was allowed to ride that jenny; mules and jennies in particular have a lot more sense than most kids and generally manage to keep both parties out of any real trouble.

Though I didn't realize it at the time, that chance of real trouble was exemplified by those candelilla wax caravans. Not that most of the people who manned them were in any way bad folks; most were much like the hardy little burros they used to transport their loads of candelilla. Quiet, unassuming, hardworking men burned dark by the relentless sun and the constant strain of a life in the middle of the harsh Chihuahuan Desert. Rather, it was the occasional dangers that dogged their trail, including those in the form of the feared Mexican *Forestales*.

A *forestale* can be best described as a hybrid cross between a park ranger and paramilitary force, armed to the teeth and with a really sour disposition to match. Their aggressive attributes were best displayed while in the pursuit of those who smuggled candelilla wax out of Coahuila and Chihuahua. You see, it was not illegal for American citizens to buy the candelilla on our side of the river, yet it was very much so for any Mexican attempting to bring the wax across.

That was why the forestales referred to our wax men as 'banditos' and why there was often a real furball going on between the two groups—sometimes on our side of the river. Both had guns; neither liked each other much, and the loss or taking of a wax load could be a life-changing event. When the two sides met and gunfire erupted, it was about the last place in the world a five-year-old kid on a worn-out jenny needed to be. After all there's nothing you can do about the bullet with your name on it, but it just makes good sense to try to avoid all those others whizzing about addressed to whomever it may concern.

One of those dustups on our side of the river occurred in the hay fields below Lajitas I was speaking of. No one was killed or even badly wounded, but "our guys" (just like a ball game where you're rooting for the home team) burned up over five hundred dollars' worth of ammunition on that one afternoon. We were certain of the amount because we were the ones supplying them with the needed firepower against what we owed them for the wax, if delivered. That's a lot of whomever-it-may-concern going every which direction, and why my grandfather didn't want me anywhere near those fields.

However, all this didn't keep me from studying that mesa for many an hour, speculating. I would venture toward it as far as I dared, telling myself that one day I would go see what was on the other side. The imagination of a small child is a powerful thing, especially when coupled with the forbidden fruit of such an impressively chiseled and ill-boding piece of ground so tantalizingly close. What made it even more tantalizing was that like a lot of other secretive spots in the Big Bend, Anguila Mesa was the subject of some wild tales and superstitions. Only lost spirits and prehistoric monsters lived up there; all others passed through at their own peril.

The "prehistoric monsters" part really gave my susceptible young mind something to play with. Like most boys my age I possessed an active interest in dinosaurs and had my personal favorites, including the pterodactyl. A comic book illustrated with World War One biplanes fighting off hordes of those "giant flying lizards" didn't help matters much. That was how I referred to them back then, as the word *pterodactyl* was darned near impossible for my preschooler tongue to pronounce. And if one of those wayward pterodactyls just happened to survive into the mid-twentieth century, then there was no better place for him to be than on top of Anguila Mesa. It was a true flight of fancy, if you will pardon the pun.

There was much more to be curious about when it came to the mesa, including a long-lasting controversy stemming from the name. *Anguila* in Spanish means eel, and most anyone would know there are no eels to be found on that particularly parched, craggy pile of jumbled rock and dirt. Some say the name was corrupted from the Spanish word for eagle, *aguila*, which would make a lot more sense. It wouldn't be the first time some pioneering cartographer got the spelling wrong for a landmark in this country, be it in Spanish or English. Others say it was named after a very old Comanche brave called Angulo. Supposedly he was the last of his people to inhabit this area, and he dwelled both on the mesa and in Santa Elena Canyon. To this day, no one seems to know what happened to this man or can document any details about him. The mystery concerning the naming of this barren piece of rock and arid soil remains unresolved.

I never made it anywhere near Anguila Mesa during those years, though I sorely wanted to go. In the interim my grandfather took me many other places in the Big Bend to marvel at or experience. As the old folks used to say, those were shining times. Yet I was not destined to set foot on that uplift until decades later, years after both of my grandparents had passed on. I suppose in a way I heeded my grandfather's warning about that mesa for as long as he was alive and then some. It's funny how things like that work out as you grow older.

Much like my grandparents, the Lajitas I knew has been gone for a long while now, replaced by a high-class tourist trap sporting condominiums, golf courses, spas, wine and cheese tours, and the like. I suppose the lowest point of all was when they built tennis courts right next to the community's graveyard. Most all of the original buildings have been demolished, though the trading post itself still stands. In recent decades it has suffered the various indignations of being a deli, a golf pro shop, a wine and espresso bar, and who knows what else to cater to the preferred clientele. I think one can understand why I don't go back to Lajitas much anymore.

Nevertheless, I was here today, at least on the very southern outskirts where the old smuggler route now serves as just another hiking trail in the national park system. These recollections of days long past filled my head as I readied myself to start up the worn path toward that same pass atop Anguila Mesa. My memories sprang from a well more than forty years old, but that massive chunk of stone still whispered in beguiling fashion to my now middle-aged ears.

Jutting up before us, the mesa appeared as enduringly formidable as it always had. Sheer rock cliffs mixed with unnavigable dry rivulets lined the rim while outsized boulders lay scattered pell-mell along the perimeters, laid open and bare to a clear blue sky which sat upon its shoulders. Coming with me were my wife as well as our two sons, who were both home from Annapolis on Christmas break. They were saddling up same as I and from time to time would stop to take it all in, gazing at what filled the southern horizon. At this distance you don't glance once and then disregard this natural anomaly; Anguila Mesa demands that you acknowledge its presence by repeatedly studying it.

It was late December and as pretty a day as one could ever hope for, especially to finally explore what had held my curiosity for so long. This is the favored time of the year to climb the mesa, as spring and summer can make for utterly brutal conditions in the blistering heat. Late August and September bring their own hazards in a completely different way; that is the rainy season and the top of Anguila Mesa is not a good place to be when a lightning storm explodes overhead. Those men who delivered the candelilla across this unyielding obstacle were hardy souls; they had to be.

We shouldered our gear and started toward the mesa on foot,

dropping into Comanche Creek. This dry wash empties into the Rio Grande less than a mile from where the old smuggling trail crosses it. Upstream not too far away the large run divides into two forks: one leading toward Contrabando Mountain while the other winds past the long-defunct Marfa and Mariposa mines and beyond to the north slope of Black Mesa. Water can occasionally be found in this channel in the form of small tinajas and intermittent springs, which come and go with the weather and time of year.

The other channel parallels the eastern slope of Lajitas Mountain. About three miles up is one of the more reliable sources of surface water for either branch. It is located along a short stretch where there is a spring of sorts and the creek has mostly a rock bottom, forming a natural bowl which forces the water to puddle and stay above ground. Most other sections, including where you cross for Anguila Mesa, have beds of dirt, sand, and gravel. The water is still there, but the porous material allows it to be hidden from view as it flows underground.

After crossing Comanche Creek, we found ourselves walking past a series of interspersed golf greens. If there is anything more out of sync than seeing a golf course in the middle of a moisture-starved land, I would be hard pressed to name the travesty. For me it was almost surreal as past clashed with present and brought to mind just how long it had been since I was five years old on the back of that jenny. Time has a way of getting past us all, even when we thought we were paying attention.

Beyond the greens, the trail splays out into several different paths running roughly parallel or crisscrossing upon themselves as they work toward the mesa. These well-worn tracks give mute testimony to how much smuggler traffic this area used to carry and may on occasion still do, though it won't be candelilla wax anymore. Trains of burros loaded down with cargo weighing 150, 200, or even more in poundage leave deep grooves in the parched soil that do not easily go away.

Anguila Mesa rises before us as we weave through the greasewood and mesquite, the crisscrossing paths combining again to prepare for the ascent into the notch situated high above. This climb goes up around six hundred feet in elevation while covering slightly more than half a mile, so it makes for a tough bit of work if you are not in proper physical conditioning. The way up is easy to spot even at a distance: half trail and half dry runoff from the saddle itself, which slashes in a zigzag pattern across the scarred, creviced face of the uplift.

We begin moving upward, admiring the stark scenery while being careful where we place our feet in traversing the more treacherous parts. This includes bits and pieces of shale rock mixed with still more shale or loose dirt scattered across the trail's surface. In places the climb is so steep that one may have to resort to all fours while scrambling up a few short, unstable stretches. Gloves are welcomed accessories, and soon enough both our gloves and footwear are covered with the scrapes and dust of our progress.

There is not a lot of foot traffic going to or from the top of Anguila Mesa, even during prime hiking periods such as now. If you like your solitude, this is a good place to be. If you are overconfident in your own abilities and do not respect this terrain for what it is, it is not a good place unless you are personally trying to validate the theory of Darwinism. There are plenty of things on or around the mesa to get you hurt and/or lost, and there is also a very good chance that no one will find you until the exact cause of your misfortune is moot.

Even on this easy lookabout we had maps, compasses, medical supplies, food, emergency stores, and water; lots of water. I cannot stress that last part enough, even during the months which most consider to be winter, at least according to the calendar. Lack of water can be a serious health hazard in any season, and the effects can come on deceptively fast. It's a lousy way to be introduced to this country no matter what time of the year.

Near the crest of the pass we turned and looked at what lay behind us. It was dry, it was desolate, and it was definitely a desert, but it was also a feast for the eyes and soul of anyone inclined toward spectacularly rugged beauty. The dull red cliffs forming the crown of Lajitas Mountain stood against the blue sky, with the foothills around it in contrasting shades of brown, gray, pink, and sand beige separated by splotches of white across the landscape. On both sides one could see the high plateaus west of Fresno Canyon and over to The Solitario, and all the way east to the Christmas Mountains. In the center entrenched amongst the flats were the tiny structures of Lajitas symbolizing a level of civilization, the life-giving river running alongside. It was an impressive view, and I thought of how welcoming it must have appeared to those wax men near the end of their long, dangerous journeys of a half century ago.

Top of Anguila Mesa with Lajitas below

But it was what lay ahead that made us catch our collective breaths and wonder if we had stepped through a portal in time somewhere along the ascent. A rugged, jumbled-up giant obstacle course of crevices, runoffs, rocky fingers, bluffs, and canyons both large and small ran for miles upon miles before us, all falling off toward the waters of the Rio Grande below. The river, making a large bend after Lajitas, swings around as a meandering avenue of reflected sunlight wandering through a rock-ribbed maze bordered by two thin green lines, each tracing the vegetation that feeds off of it. These were the only real areas of green to be found for as far as the eye could see.

From here one can observe how the massive Anguila Mesa is only the northernmost portion of a far greater uplift known as the Sierra Ponce. This striking perspective also makes one ponder the geological forces which caused the Rio Grande to somehow lodge itself in the midst of such a range and now serve as a natural marker between Texas and Old Mexico. How it managed to do so from Lajitas to the mouth of Santa Elena Canyon is something that boggles one's comprehension of how this land must have come into being.

But there is more, far more to the story of this country if one knows why and where to look. On the horizon to the southwest

Looking toward San Carlos Estado de Chihuahua

is another sierra which shields the historic Chihuahuan pueblo of San Carlos. According to the Mexican government, this community was renamed 'Manuel Benavides' back in the 1930s to honor a hero of the Great Mexican Revolution. Though this occurred some eighty years ago, the village is still called San Carlos by many of its inhabitants. Such continuing traditions give one a general idea of how much sway the central government in faraway Mexico City often has over these proud, hardy *gente de la frontera*.

Perhaps their recalcitrance comes by their hard-won heritage from the nearby Presidio de San Carlos, first established before the American Revolution. It was envisioned, constructed, and commanded by famed Spanish officer and future military governor of Texas Brigadier General Hugo Oconór, a redheaded Irish expatriate of royal lineage who was born Hugh O'Conor and became known to the Apaches as *El Capitan Rojo*. A man of substantial personal charisma and leadership traits, his efforts at San Carlos as well as nearby San Vicente were an attempt to bring some semblance of Spain's rule over this forbidding country known then as the *Tierra Despoblado*.

But the trouble was the land wasn't uninhabited, and the numerous marauding Comanche and Apache bands which roamed this region made that point abundantly clear. These predatory Native Americans also made it clear they did not appreciate any foreign interlopers intruding into their internecine raiding upon each other. The hapless Spanish settlers who ventured here faced these combined depredations and fury visited upon them time and again, and thus the need for men such as Hugo Oconór and his military presidios. The resulting three-way vicious rounds of attacks and counterattacks went on for decades. In the interim Spanish rule gave way to Mexican sovereignty, but the fighting continued, reaching further intensity as the newly formed Republic of Texas pushed both Comanches and Apaches further southwest toward Mexico.

Often enough it was the Comanches who held the upper hand in all this. Stories abound of the Comanches, led by their prophetess Tave Pete, riding their ponies in regal fashion through the middle of San Carlos, the Mexicans virtually powerless to stop them. Tave Pete was the grandmother of the great Comanche Chief Tave Tuk. His Spanish name was *Bajo Del Sol*, given to him because he was afraid of nothing "Under the Sun." If there ever was a name which better exemplified the ferocity and raw courage of the Comanche warrior, this had to be it. Life can be a mite uncomfortable in the Big Bend Country of the twenty-first century, but by comparison it was often very short and brutal when Tave Pete and Bajo Del Sol were on the prowl.

Even now, some 250 years later, El Despoblado still appears to be empty. From our vantage point, as far as our eyes could take us to the south, east, and west, there was no hint of man, Comanche or otherwise. The untold numbers of forgotten souls who had lived and died within our purview had left no more visible mark upon the land than melted snow at the close of a warm spring day. A kind of reverence swelled up within; it had taken me over forty years to get here, yet from where I stood it was obvious it had been worth the wait.

This was not to be one of our usual exploratory jaunts covering a large swath of territory; Cathy was unable to do much more physically, as the climb had taken its toll on her. But we did want to take a closer look around, so she made the pragmatic decision to set up a hasty camp along one side of the saddle while the rest of us set off in different directions on top of the mesa.

While Levi scouted northwest along the ridge and Ethan worked his way to the southeast, I set a southerly course toward

Downriver and on to Santa Elena Canyon

the nearest part of the river. My first impression was quickly rein-
forced as to the graphic ruggedness of my new surroundings; one
could not go far this direction before being met by topographical
challenges which lay in rows of solid rock and vertical surfaces
stacked atop each other. Below my position was a bluff going
on for miles, the face of it standing several hundred feet in most
spots. Its upper end peters out near the elbow of the river below
Lajitas, close to where some abandoned structures have sat decaying for as long as I can remember.

I also knew of a trail that once came off the river directly below
me and another paralleling the foot of this shelf, but I couldn't
see either of them from my perch above. This fact underlines just
how rough the terrain actually is and brings up another bit of
advice I have given many times and which needs to be repeated
here: There are reasons for the main traveled trails atop Anguila
Mesa; stay on them. Unless you have been up here many times
and can read a quad map like it was your own personal diary,
remain close to these paths. What at first seems to be easily navigable ground contains hidden pitfalls which become even larger
and more perilous the closer you get to the river.

Almost all of the man-made routes across Anguila Mesa were
created for the moving of goods and supplies from one point to

the other. Mostly those were smuggled goods and supplies, which made the journey even more dangerous and unpredictable. No matter if they were smuggling livestock, guns, liquor, candelilla wax, or dope, there was no profit to be made if their cargo had to be abandoned or was lost along the way. Unlike many who venture across the mesa now, these men weren't up here for the fun of it. Many of them might have been smugglers, bandits, and thieves, but that doesn't mean they were stupid, and they treasured their own lives and welfare as much as any other person. They also knew this country better than anyone else could ever hope to. Such knowledge was a closely guarded secret for their continued good health and livelihood, and these trails helped minimize the numerous dangers inherent to their trade.

There are a far larger number of such trails crisscrossing this uplift than many at first glance would think possible. The basic, better-known routes would include the one along the river and around the mesa, the one through the saddle, the zigzag route off the northeast shoulder past Tinaja Lujan, and the favored smugglers' path from *Cañon de Bosque* in Mexico. You can look upon them as lifelines flung across this unfrequented slice of the Chihuahuan Desert, courtesy of those who came before.

The more cautious candelilla smugglers preferred to travel downriver from the mouth of Cañon de Bosque before crossing and climbing up through the saddle, rather than utilizing the easier trails which ran upriver or traversed it at the elbow below Lajitas. Both of the latter routes kept them precariously close to the Mexican side for some distance in more or less open country, which was the main cause leading to the aforementioned gun battle in our hay fields. The temptation for those *forestales* upon seeing their quarry so close and only separated by that thin ribbon of brown water proved to be too much to bear. The smugglers' path up through the saddle was longer, drier, and far more challenging to navigate, but for their use the harder route was the more prudent one.

Along with the jagged, broken landscape and environmental extremes found on Anguila Mesa, there is also the question of water. The only natural sources on top are the tinajas such as the Lujan and the Blanca, along with some smaller, unnamed ones. To my knowledge there are no springs, and the tinajas can be very much of a hit and miss affair. Even if there is water present in them, it might not be any good. The other part in this situation to be accounted for is accessibility. Many of these natural rock basins can be hard to get to, especially during the drier months. In effect that is why you will find water in them to begin with: they are emplaced in such a manner as to be sheltered from sun and wind, making for a very slow evaporation rate. The flipside to this is some of these tinajas can be somewhat difficult, even precarious to get to.

As most anyone can discern for themselves. the most reliable of all water sources is the river, which in turn presents yet another catch-22. You can stand in many spots on the mesa and see it plainly, sometimes from only a couple hundred yards away. Yet that short distance usually entails an equivalent drop in elevation, much of it straight down. Suffice to say that when you go to Anguila Mesa, the wise thing to do is bring your own water in amounts exceeding what you think you might need. It's a lonely, out-of-the-way place. But who knows, you might come across some poor soul who did not heed this advice.

Come around lunch time we met back where Cathy was encamped near the top of the saddle. The three of us grabbed a rocky seat beside her and broke open our food stores, eating and telling of what we had seen. Everyone's perspective was somewhat different due to our dissimilar approaches and directions. Yet one observation remained a constant: Anguila Mesa was not like any other locale we had seen in the Big Bend or anywhere else. It had its own singularity, its own "feel" for lack of a better word. Call it what you will; something just seemed to reach down deep inside in a uniquely primal way.

After hearing us visit about our experiences and taking an extended breather, Cathy declared herself sufficiently rested to do a little sightseeing herself. We finished our meal and let her lead off across the mesa, seeing everything anew as she felt led toward still other spots than those we had visited.

Along the way we could view both Canyon Flag and La Mariposa from afar, the so-called *mesitas* which sit atop the eastern side of the hulking escarpment. *La Mariposa* means the Butterfly, and was named such due to its supposedly similar shape when observed from the air. This *La Mariposa* is not to be confused with the old Marfa and Mariposa mines situated at the foot of California Mountain, some six miles to the north of Anguila Mesa. Those mines were the beginning of the great cinnabar rush in this country, a veritable bonanza which had nothing to do with this unusual landmark.

We wandered about somewhat aimlessly for the next few hours, not really getting anyplace but filled with wonderment at what we saw. Everywhere you looked there was something that appeared unusual, even bizarre. It was like strolling through a three-dimensional jigsaw puzzle a small child had thrown into the air out of frustration and then stomped on for good measure. The comic strip character Alley Oop and his pet dinosaur 'Dinny' would have felt right at home here.

Too soon for our liking, we were back at the top of the pass. While Cathy took another break before our returning descent to Lajitas, the rest of us continued to soak in as much as we possibly could from this brief trip. Standing on the boulder-strewn ridge just west of the saddle itself, my younger son Ethan and I took a long last look together.

As we turned to go he said to me in a joking fashion; "You know, Dad, this would be the perfect place for a Pterodactyl farm."

His words stopped me cold in midstride. My mind spun back over the decades to a skinny little five-year-old kid who had shared much the same opinion. That was a long time ago, but for a magical moment I was sitting on the front porch of the trading post again, staring hard at where we now stood, my budding imagination working overtime. I could also see my grandmother using her hand to shield her eyes from the afternoon sun, watching.

I looked at Ethan, his lean frame silhouetted against the desert terrain falling away behind him. Though only nineteen years of age, he was already a man to be reckoned with who possessed that equally rare gift of not taking himself too seriously. The genes run strong in my family across the generations, and against such a backdrop I saw many who had long since departed, including my grandmother. He had that same sly, easygoing grin and twinkle in his eye which reminded me so much of her and her zest for living.

"Yeah it would be, wouldn't it?" and I grinned back, savoring those childhood memories for as long as I possibly could, knowing that they would all melt away again far too quickly.

And then they did.

CHAPTER 2

Thirst!

This desert is like being in love
with a beautiful woman who is
always trying to kill you.

—ANONYMOUS

When my sons came home during their years at Annapolis, they
often did not do so alone. For some reason many of their fellow
midshipmen reveled in coming to West Texas and seeing how
the "other half" lived, so to speak. It was a new world for them,
and made us appreciate even more what we have in our own
back yard. Whenever possible we would take our guests with us
on trips to the Big Bend. Each of these forays were unique and
memorable for their own reasons, but especially so this time
around.

My older son Levi wanted to lead this particular expedition,
and I gave him the full responsibility in doing so. He took care of
all the planning and preparations, scheduling us a backpacking
trip which would begin in the Chisos Basin and move up the trail
for Laguna Meadows. Once past that point we would veer onto
the Blue Creek Canyon Trail and stay on it to the terminus at the
old Homer Wilson ranch headquarters. From there we would
follow the Dodson Trail and move east below the south face of
the Chisos Mountains.

Up to this point we would be traveling along what the park
officials refer to as the Outer Mountain Loop. But once we got to
where Elephant Tusk Trail branched off the Dodson, we would
follow the Elephant Tusk route until it intersected Fresno Creek.
An explanatory note for those who may be confused: there are
two *Fresno* (Spanish for *ash tree*) Creeks of note in this area; one

in the national park and another located in the Big Bend Ranch State Park. There are others of the same name in the Big Bend, but these two are by far the best known and recalled.

Our four-man party would snake its way down this particular Fresno Creek until we were out of the higher country. From there we would set course for Glenn Spring, then head northwesterly through Robber's Roost, hit the Juniper Canyon Trail, and then begin climbing in earnest again until it teed into the trail for Boot Canyon. At that junction we would ascend up to the Pinnacles before ultimately finishing where we had started, in the Chisos Basin. It was an ambitious plan, with close to fifty miles of back-packing to be done in four days. Yet Levi had researched it thoroughly, and we had a good crew. I had never personally been on the Dodson before, nor in the Fresno or Elephant Tusk areas. This was going to be as new for me as anyone else.

My confederates in this endeavor would consist of Levi, myself, and two of his Naval Academy classmates—Joe Gehrz and David Flannery. I had met these two young men during their prior visits to our home and had taken a liking to both. Joe was from Minnesota and was an experienced outdoorsman of some skill in his part of the world. David was a San Antonio native who had never done much when it came to being in the wild; this would be his first exposure to it. Neither had ever been to the Big Bend before, and both were new to the desert. There was also a single note of concern: David had recently gone through a bout of mononucleosis. Though he said he was fine and appeared quite fit, I still made a mental note for possible future reference.

The first afternoon upon arriving at the park we divided into two teams and drove out to emplace the caches of water and provisions that we would need along our path. Joe and Levi put theirs along the Dodson Trail near Carousel Mountain while David and I stashed ours just north of Glenn Spring. I took the time to acquaint David with the general area as well as needed landmarks in case he had to find the site on his own. This would prove to be a prescient decision on my part.

We spent our first night at Dugout Wells, making a cold camp off the road from where we parked the vehicles. It was that time of year when the nights could be below freezing, but the following day punishingly hot in the lower elevations. This night proved to be no exception to the rule; David and Joe began learning the lessons on the environmental extremes which can be found in the

Big Bend, and how to deal with them.

Before first light next morning we were up and moving around, partly due to the definite chill which had permeated our bedrolls. After downing a quick breakfast, we broke camp and drove to our launch point in the Chisos Basin. Following a final check of our equipment and route, we saddled up with our packs and set out for Laguna Meadows.

The climb from the Basin to Laguna Meadows is one which I have made several times before, yet I never find it less of a thrill to the senses. The cold air was crisp in the early morning, the sun bright as it rose in the eastern sky, and impatience was brimming in my fellow adventurers to see what lay over yonder mountain. I knew exactly how they felt, as that very same sensation was also pulling me forward. It was a glorious day to be alive and headed for the back country as we passed through stands of live oak and juniper, mixed with the occasional mesquite along with examples of native cacti.

There were plenty of other people around us on the beginning of this first leg, but the higher we zigzagged our way up the more infrequent they became. By the time we hit the turnoff for Blue Creek Canyon Trail, the flow of humanity had reduced itself to a trickle, and later that day this trickle would play out along the Dodson. From then forward it would be two more days and many more miles before we would see another human being.

The head of the trail for Blue Creek Canyon is nearly 6800 feet high, and the trail runs mostly downhill all the way to the old Homer Wilson headquarters, located near the present-day Ross Maxwell Scenic Drive. You turn off Laguna Meadows below Emory Peak, its fractured cliffs perched another thousand feet above your left shoulder. This peak is the highest point in the Chisos Mountains range and one of the tallest in the state of Texas. One can hike up to its very summit if you choose to do so; the view is absolutely spectacular from there at any heading on a compass.

Working our way down Blue Creek Canyon, we could see the vestiges of the wildfire which swept through this area in early 1989. It is not hard to spot the rotted stumps of trees which once grew here, even as younger vegetation struggles to shroud the damage done. There is a marker commemorating the event on the South Rim Trail at a spot overlooking the canyon. This fire was reportedly caused by humans, and left a lot of scarred and blackened earth in its wake. In the mountainous desert area of

Emory Peak

the Big Bend, those scars take a long time to heal. It was only because of the dogged efforts of hundreds of firefighters, park rangers, and civilian volunteers that the carnage was not far worse.

With the ground sloping away and still being first-day fresh, we made good time along this portion of our trip. The chilly morning prior had given birth to a truly beautiful day, and the skies were absolutely as clear and blue as one could possibly imagine. This made for some simply spectacular imagery which no camera can ever begin to fully capture. But we tried all the same as our eyes took in the visual feast which Blue Creek Canyon presented us.

Meanwhile we continued to be on the move, putting miles and distance behind us as the high country greenery rapidly gave way to the mesquite, greasewood, and cacti of the lower elevations. Even the rock itself changed; almost a mile up from the ruins of the old ranch we came across eroded red rock forming fantastic shapes known as "hoodoos" in other parts of the American Southwest. No matter what you may have in mind for extravagant scenery, there is likely a little bit of it to be found someplace within the Big Bend.

By late afternoon we were at the headquarters of what had been the Homer Wilson ranch and took a bit of a break to al-

Looking west from Dodson Trail

low Joe and David the opportunity to look around. Once their curiosity was satiated we pushed on, now on the Dodson Trail, and headed toward our replenishment cache at the foot of Carousel Mountain. Levi and Joe said they picked a good spot for the cache, and had camouflaged it well. That was a good thing because when we got there it was about a hundred feet from a Boy Scout camp.

Nonchalantly we gathered up our provisions as the surprised scouts looked on, not certain of what to say or do about these four desert apparitions which had appeared out of nowhere and seemed bent upon returning to the same. After loading up on MREs and water, we waved a friendly goodbye to our baffled young audience and began following the Dodson as it snaked its lonely way east along the bottom side of the Chisos. The shadows were growing long and a chilliness was coming back to the arid air when we found a likely spot to camp for the night. After a meal and some talk about what we had seen that day, we turned in with our thoughts upon what lay ahead tomorrow.

The next morning turned out even colder than the one before, which probably had something to do with the increase in elevation compared to Dugout Wells. Again we were up at the crack of dawn, moving around stiffly in the frigid air and trying to warm our trail-worn bodies. Each of us looked expectantly to the east, wishing for the sun to rise above the peaks and melt the persistent chill from our bones. Yet there was many a mountain between us and the brightening glow announcing sunrise, so after a quick breakfast we geared up and started along the Dodson again. If the sun was running late due to the intervening high ground, we would go and seek it out ourselves.

I took the point, followed by David and then Joe with Levi bringing up the rear. Each of us was hitting his rhythm, making individual contributions to the betterment of the team we formed. Levi was in overall charge, consulting his compass and topographical maps to keep a tally of our progress and advise on what lay ahead. Joe carried the extra water and rations from our cache below Carousel Mountain, and as an aspiring Navy doctor handled any first aid needs. David, being new to this game, was not given any responsibilities other than taking care of his gear and making copious mental notes as he learned of life on the trail. He was working hard at it, too, and it was a special time for me to see this country anew through his wide-open eyes.

Eastward and upward we ascended, steadily gaining in both mileage and altitude. Sloping away behind us to the west one could see Mule Ears, Santa Elena Canyon, and a large chunk of *el Estado de Chihuahua* in the distance. Meanwhile the sun began to shine with full effect and the morning quickly turned from pleasant to hot as we climbed on. That is the way of the desert and of the Big Bend; extremes are found in so many ways no matter where you go or what time of day or year it is. It is part and parcel of the enduring magic of this land.

That magic can be a double-edged sword in the more desolate parts of this region. The Dodson Trail is only for those with the physical stamina and experience to make the trip, and few of the millions who have visited the park ever try themselves along this route. People have died out here and in the surrounding canyons and badlands in overreaching themselves and their capabilities. The traditional Spanish word for caution, *cuidado*, is also regional Mexican slang meaning "be careful" or "pay attention"— a phrase to be kept in mind by any prudent sojourner passing though.

Our path continued on eastwardly, entering a series of ups and downs as morning wore on to noon. From time to time we observed signs of humankind from another era, long before this was national park land. There was an old fence line and a gap, its wire gate long since removed and carried off for some unknown purpose. The remains of a corral were spotted off the trail to the north, as well as other dilapidated sentries of wire and post which appeared to have once formed a long-defunct horse trap. Farther to the north the massive south rim of the Chisos rose high above us, reaching up for the vividly blue sky that framed its features. The word *magnificent* does not even begin to describe the breathtaking views we saw that morning.

On the northern edge of the Sierra Quemada, Dodson Trail eases through an unnamed pass which marks the high point of the route at some 5200 feet in elevation. It is also where you leave the panoramas and various landmarks of the southwestern side of the park and are exposed to those on the opposite side of the divide. In the distance you begin to see Elephant Tusk, Tortuga Mountain, the Chilicotal, and all the way to the Sierra Del Carmen and into *el Estado de Coahuila*. Natural rock formations created by a combination of seismic activity and erosion look almost like manmade walls as they run down and away from us, nearly as straight as arrows and only interrupted by the numerous arroyos and crevices carved out of the landscape. We walk and marvel at what is to be observed in every direction. To see this one stretch of rugged territory spilling off the south side of the Chisos was worth the entire trip in itself.

Taking the Elephant Tusk Trail cutoff which runs southeast from the Dodson, our little group ambled along as we put our backs into it and enjoyed the scenery. Things were going well; we still had plenty of water, our next cache was not that far away, the weather was beautiful, and we were running ahead of schedule. But like I said before, this country is rife with all manner of extremities, some of which we would experience in the very near future.

Elephant Tusk Trail is not as well marked as the Dodson and harder to navigate. In fact, there are portions of it which are giving way to the ravages of exposure, time, and lack of foot traffic. More than anything else, it has reverted to being a game trail marked occasionally by rock cairns as it crawls hither and yon toward Elephant Tusk Peak. It is not a trail for the novice; I strongly recommend that one has knowledge of both map and compass, be in excellent physical condition, and avoid the hot season if you decide to try it.

Moving down Elephant Tusk Trail from the Dodson

But there is a flipside to all that, because if you do go, you will experience a vital part of the Big Bend National Park which so many others cannot even begin to imagine. There is something about traveling a faint trail where few others have gone before that gives a special meaning to life and what we get out of it. Inside most of mankind is a hardwired need for this sort of journey through nature which must be attended to on occasion, albeit infrequently for the great majority of us. Elephant Tusk is one of those trails which satisfies that need in a manner going beyond written word or spoken expression.

About a mile and a half from its teeing off the Dodson, the trail drops into Fresno Creek. It was there we came across some welcome shade from the hot sun and took a late lunch break. Once satisfied and refreshed, our party pushed down the creek toward the point where we would climb out and head for Glenn Spring. Though not very big in size, Fresno Creek is another one of those places that makes for a memorable trek. Winding down from the base of the South Rim, this small canyon has been known to be a reliable water source for as long as man has traveled in this area. Even during blistering weather and drought, water can be found in the mountainous sections of this crevice, which continues past

Head of Fresno Creek below the Chisos

Mariscal Mine before ultimately dumping into the Rio Grande near the Solis.

A word should be mentioned here concerning the springs marked on the quad maps for this area: many of those springs are in reality tinajas. A *tinaja* can be best described as a natural holding spot for standing pools of water, usually in rocky basins where it cannot leech underground. Water found in a tinaja might have been sitting there for weeks or even months, depending on the seasonal rains. In contrast a spring is where water comes to the surface from somewhere underground and usually has a flow to it which helps purify the contents.

In Fresno Creek there are both. The biggest and most recognizable of these is what the National Park Service refers to as Hop Springs and Skip and Jump Tinajas. The names are somewhat apt, but cumbersome. Colloquially, these three are combined and known as "the Waterworks." This is yet another one of those extremes one finds so often while exploring this country. One might never believe that such an oasis exists when standing only a few hundred yards away on higher ground. There is little greenery to give it away; the canyon floor is made up mostly of massive slabs of rock where nothing can grow. This also forces the water to stay above ground at least for a short distance before it disappears again into the beds of gravel downstream.

We stopped again to enjoy these inviting pools of the desert's most precious resource, pulling our boots and socks off to soak our feet. It was so cool, so invigorating. As was our habit we checked our water rations; there was still an adequate supply and we elected not to fill up at an unpurified source. Joe, our resident medical student, was leery of the water's appearance as well as the number of little critters swimming around in it. After all, we were only a little over six miles as the crow flies from our next cache, and no one saw the need to expose himself to the effects of possible bad water. Looking back, I knew we were rolling the dice by not filling up again; it was a mistake mostly on my part, because I should have known better.

Our little group saddled up and moved on downstream; the elevation loss becoming more pronounced as the bottom became narrower and the canyon walls higher. A couple of times we had to navigate past sudden drop-offs in the canyon floor, but nothing that slowed us down much or gave pause for second thoughts. Our main concern was slipping on the slick rock while maneuvering with the extra weight on our backs.

I was pulling point when I came around a narrow bend amid smoothed rock formations caused by eons of cascading flash floods. In the middle of this was a natural chokepoint, formed by solid rock vees angling in from either side that nearly touched at the canyon floor. Just beyond the base of the vee was the top of a cottonwood tree, signaling a fair sized drop with no easy way of circumventing it. This was my first indication that things were about to go wrong.

I came to a halt and called out over my shoulder; "I think we have a problem."

Levi came forward at a recon shuffle and took in what was before him. "Uh-oh," was all he said, as he unshouldered his gear and gingerly made his way into the vee while the rest of us dropped packs and followed him in.

Together the four of us examined the drop-off. There were several other variations of Levi's "uh-oh" which were voiced upon full comprehension of this unexpected monkey wrench, as well as some more colorful phrases which were well suited to the event.

Our ages-old new opponent was not very deep but just damp enough to make its polished rock surface slick as glass. Combined with the weight of our gear and the way we would traverse it, the descent was an open invitation to someone getting hurt. Levi was not happy; his information stated the canyon was navigable throughout its course. Perhaps so at a different time without packs, but not here, not now. If we made the attempt and someone fell and injured himself, we were a long way from any outside help.

Faced with this complication, Levi broke out his quad map and unfolded it on the crevice's floor as we discussed our alternatives. We could return up the Fresno to the Dodson and on to the Basin through Juniper Canyon and the Pinnacles, thereby completing the Outer Mountain Loop as a consolation prize. But that route would leave us low on provisions, and more importantly water, even if we filled up at Dodson Spring or one of the tinajas above us in Fresno Creek.

Our second option was to climb out and guide back on to Elephant Tusk Trail, follow it down to Black Gap Road and then up to Glenn Spring. It would be a long haul to our water and provisions cache, but it would put us back on track to finish out our original route. It was also an area we knew something about, and the natural water source at Glenn Spring was very reliable. This was the alternative we went for.

The first order of business was to get out of the canyon, which presented another appreciable difficulty due to its steep, often vertical walls. Levi studied the contour lines on his map and decided to backtrack about half a mile to where we stood a chance of being able to climb our way out. I remembered seeing the spot he had in mind when we passed through, and concurred with his hastily planned detour. We reversed direction and began working our way back up the Fresno.

The selected spot proved to be a tough ascent which took up more time and even more energy. Both were spent in using not only our legs but also our hands as we literally clawed our way out of the crevice, grasping at every bit of sparse vegetation available in pulling ourselves upwards. I was huffing like a tired old steam engine pulling a steep grade when we finally intersected Elephant Tusk Trail. It was a not-so-gentle reminder that it had been over thirty years since I was a grunt in the Marines and that none of us ever get any younger.

Once above the Fresno we could see the singularly shaped mountain called Elephant Tusk, which a century ago was known

Negotiating a part of Elephant Tusk Trail

as Indianola Peak. Whoever was responsible for the renaming must have gotten the tusk of a rhinoceros mixed up with that of an elephant, because this particular terrain feature far more resembles the former. From here forward and into the next day, its distinctive shape would serve as a quick reference point in orienting ourselves as we moved along. It would also serve as a persistent warning flag that our detour was leading us south by southeast and mostly away from our cache at Glenn Spring. By the time we were through, those six miles as the crow flies would turn into nearly fifteen on the ground, with not an easy one to be found in the bunch.

After Elephant Tusk Trail leaves Fresno Creek the path becomes very much a hit-or-miss affair. Rock cairns are only occasional; very few people utilize this route, which has led to its ensuing decay and "hairing over." Some stretches of the route have simply eroded away into nothingness; we came upon one spot at the edge of a drop-off where the trail just flat disappeared. Down below, about two hundred feet away, one could plainly see it start off again. We wasted some time looking around for someplace where it might zig-zag off the high ground, but there wasn't any. So straight off we went, sliding on all fours as well as our butts to get to the bottom.

The shadowy fingers of late afternoon were stretching out before us when the faint trail entered an unnamed canyon skirting the north side of Elephant Tusk. It was not as large nor as deep as the one which contained Fresno Creek, but it was as rough as corn cob with several narrows and sharp drop-offs which had to be negotiated. We made our way through safely, but it did a good job of eating up even more time and effort, and by now the sun had gone down.

Levi's quad map notated a spring ahead, and as we drew closer one could observe a small copse of trees and underbrush signaling some promise of water. We scoured about looking to replenish our canteens, but there was only a mere seep oozing up through the mud, choked with weeds and brush with minute dabs of stagnant water interspersed among the overgrowth. Sometimes no water is better than bad water, so we passed and pushed on to find even more drop-offs and narrows. Each one in turn slowed us down as we sought a way to maneuver around in the darkness that was enveloping us. At least we didn't have to be concerned about losing the trail at this juncture; there was no place else for it to go.

Our little party moved on resolutely, taking advantage of the coolness of the night to gain distance and avoid the heat of the day to come. Our water situation dictated that we make maximum use of every environmental advantage from this point forward. Today it had been quite warm for this higher elevation and time of year, and something was telling me that tomorrow would be boiling hot in the lower flats south of Glenn Spring.

There was no moon, and we only had the starlight that managed to enter the deep gloom of the cut to guide by. Somewhere in the blackness the trail climbed out of the canyon, but we did not note its departing. The bottom of the crevice had opened up and made for much easier walking as we shuffled along in single file. Already familiar with the condition of the trail, we reasoned that trying to find and then follow it on such a dark night would be an exercise in utter frustration.

But it was also so black inside the gorge that one sometimes took a step forward partly on faith because of the limited visibility. Though the canyon floor had flattened out somewhat, there were still small drops and loose rock formations that we had to ply our way through. The sound of a man stumbling in the dark with some fifty-odd extra pounds on his back is not a comforting thing.

After a couple of such episodes which culminated in David nearly falling completely face down, I called for a halt and we talked the situation over. The lack of ambient light meant there was too much of a chance of someone injuring himself and not being able to go any farther, which could be a far more dangerous circumstance than what we were currently facing. We were still a long way from any outside help or assistance if the need arose.

Levi agreed and said the moon was supposed to rise shortly after three in the morning. We decided to make a cold camp where we stood, and once the moon was up to begin pushing forward again. This would give us several hours of relative coolness to travel in before tomorrow's heat hit in force, and by that time we should be nearly to Glenn Spring and our next cache. I made a small meal out of the MREs in my pack and washed it down with water from my last canteen; a canteen which was nigh empty.

I did not say anything about that. The last bit of our prior cache of water was in Joe's pack. I figured that he and David needed the lion's share of what remained, as they were still not fully acclimated and David was coming off his bout with mono. Little did I know that Levi was thinking and doing the very same thing. Within the next sixteen hours, both of us would experience the debilitating effects of dehydration as we had never done before.

Half sitting, half lying down with my ALICE pack still strapped to my shoulders, I positioned myself so the moon's light would hit me square in the face as soon as it peeped over the canyon wall. It would be enough to awaken me from a light sleep and we would be off again, but now with some illumination to guide by. The night was pleasant, even restful, and I drifted off thinking about what must be done tomorrow.

As anticipated, the moon rose over the rim and immediately its brightness snapped me back to full consciousness. But my internal clock was saying that something was very wrong and with a sinking feeling I checked my wristwatch; it read 6:03 a.m. None of us had calculated the fact that moonrise was determined at a certain elevation while on flat, open ground; not inside a small canyon with steep walls close about.

Coming to my feet I began urging everyone else to wake up, that we were already way behind schedule. Though trail-weary and a bit bleary-eyed, the other three were on their feet almost immediately and began making ready to go. As we inhaled a hurried breakfast I instructed them to wash it down with whatever water they might still have on them. The day was shaping up to be really hot, and that water wasn't going to do them any good swishing around in their canteens. In a little over ten minutes we were headed out again.

The cool of the early morning was refreshing as Levi calculated the best route to get us where we needed to be. His idea was to stick with the canyon bottom until it entered flatter terrain and he could shoot an azimuth for the area just south of Glenn Spring. The reasoning was sound; the walls around us were still steep and would demand valuable time and effort to overcome. As we walked down the gorge, it quickly became a draw and we selected a likely spot to leave it. Levi oriented his map, called out the landmarks to guide by, and started us off in an easterly direction. I was pulling point again.

At first we made good progress before being slowed down by large intersecting arroyos mixed with small seas of lechuguilla. *Lechuguilla*, or "Spanish Dagger" as it is often called, can be problematic to traverse when in such abundance. These clumps of tough, leather-like splines might be looked upon as Mother Nature's equivalent to punji stakes and can be just as effective. I have seen lechuguilla cripple horses, cattle, burros, and more than one human being with a misplaced step or lack of caution when encountering it. Your best bet is to zigzag your way across to avoid the thicker patches. This slowed us down even further and added distance to our accompanying loss of time.

It was then the sun came over Talley Mountain and things took a definite turn for the worse. There are certain days in the lower parts of the Big Bend, no matter what time of year, where the prevailing environmental factors combine for a lethal, scorching heat. After you have been in this country for a while, you can sense one of those days coming. The wildlife usually present in the early hours of morning act differently; there is no wind, no cloud in the sky; nothing to keep the desert from becoming an all-consuming inferno. When the sun rises on such a morning the effect is almost immediate and is much like opening the door to an oven. And like an oven, it begins to cook most anything inside it.

This prescience about the coming day had lingered in my consciousness since the evening before. I knew what to expect, yet that burning orb's presence on the eastern horizon put an ominous exclamation mark to our present circumstance. Sweat began to form and pool in every pore, precious moisture which our bodies had to use to maintain proper internal temperatures. But once that moisture is spent, it needs regeneration, and we had nothing left in our water bags with which to do so.

Adding to this witches' brew of real trouble was the very nature of the land itself. The constant crossing of arroyos found in the rugged terrain on this side of the Chisos, along with the acres upon acres of lechuguilla, was forcing us to swing to the south and away from a more direct path to Glenn Spring. Faced with this new twist Levi recalculated a different heading, one aiming straight for where Black Gap Road ran closest to our current position. We plodded on toward the rising sun, guiding upon the southern peak of Talley Mountain, which was growing oh so slowly larger in front of us.

Through the desert flats of lechuguilla and across the intersecting arroyos we kept to our pace, now in search of an outreaching elbow to a primitive road which would lead us to our destination. Levi's map and compass skills were nearly perfect; we hit Black Gap Road precisely at the point we had wanted to. Now began the five final miles to our water and provisions located just north of Glenn Spring. We were already tired, thirsty, and encrusted with dried sweat, and it was also getting hotter, a lot hotter.

As the sun rose higher in the sky and we continued on, I could see the beginning stages of dehydration begin to take its toll. Joe and David, who had been allowed to consume more of our water supply, were not suffering near as much as Levi and I were. It was only then I learned that Levi had done the same thing I had and for the same reasons: gone easy on the water so the other two could have more.

We held a quick conference as we trudged along, not wanting to stop. Stopping was the last thing we needed to do, and all of us knew why. It was decided we would break into two groups; Joe and David being far fresher would step it out towards our cache at Glenn Spring. David knew where the water and provisions had been emplaced, and I had made certain at the time he could find them on his own. That little bit of extra preparation was going to pay off.

I was concerned about our evolving predicament but not particularly worried, as I knew we would make it. However, the remaining distance to be covered was going to be a gut check for everyone involved. My main goal was to keep anything else untoward from happening until we had safely moved into the Glenn Spring area and obtained our waiting provisions. Before they started out I admonished both Joe and David to stay on Black Gap Road until reaching Glenn Spring, no matter what they saw or heard, or *thought* they saw and heard. Though it was obvious they were better hydrated, I knew from prior experience that a lack of water hits particularly hard and fast on those who are not used to high temperatures or who have been recently ill.

Acute dehydration can cause a sudden onslaught of maladies, including hallucinations; I had seen this happen many years ago in the Marine Corps while involved in a training exercise on the island of Aruba. A forced march or "hump" had been scheduled immediately following our arrival. The weather had been hot, but more importantly we had just gotten off ship and were not acclimated to the environment. Furthermore, no orders were given for water breaks or specified amounts to be consumed during the exercise. We ended up with several cases of dehydration, heat exhaustion, and one full-fledged heat stroke casualty which got everyone's attention.

After the incident I asked a Navy doc about the strange hallucinations some of the men experienced. He explained by saying our brains work by electrical synapses, and these synapses need a certain amount of bodily water to fire correctly. Take that water away and those synapses begin to misfire and short out, much like a set of frayed spark plug wires on an automobile engine. This is what causes the hallucinations and why they seem so real to those suffering from them. To a minor degree they can happen quite early in the dehydration process, depending upon the individual. It is also a condition which takes some time to recuperate from. Much like carbon monoxide poisoning, you don't immediately bounce back once exposed to fresh air.

As for myself, I was just going to have to take it a little slower than the rest; you might think upon it as the classical battle between the vigor of youth and the experience of age. Experience had better prepared me for what might lay ahead, though I must admit to feeling less than the complete man as Joe and David began to outpace me. Then I realized they were both in prime physical condition and I was old enough to be their grandfather. I don't know if those pertinent facts made me feel much better, but they were facts that had to be lived with.

Levi hung back at my side, even after I advised him to go on

Desert terrain south of Glenn Spring

with Joe and David. My older son was a former cross-country state champion, and when it came to pure physical conditioning, he was in the best shape of all. I knew that I was holding him up and could also tell that he was more concerned about me than I could ever be about myself. At one point he suggested I find a place to rest and he would go on to Glenn Spring to bring back some water. I remember looking around at the bleak landscape literally radiating with heat and mildly inquiring, "And just where do you think that might be?"

And it got hotter still. Levi was also worried about his friends and their unfamiliarity with the area. Finally he was convinced enough to go on, promising to get water back to me as quickly as possible. I had him make the same commitment as the other two: whatever you see and hear, whatever you *think* you see and hear, stay on the road. Like Joe and David, he soon began to make distance on me and within a short time all three had pulled far enough ahead to be out of sight. I continued at my same pace, concentrating on putting one foot in front of the other to reach our destination.

I was also watching the boot prints left by those in front of me. Someone once remarked that a man's footprint can be as individual as his fingerprint, and that is not too far from the truth. After the past few days I could easily differentiate between the three. Monitoring their tracks was one of my main responsibilities if I had to bring up the rear.

Everything looked good until reaching a large draw which crossed the track we were on. That was where Levi's boot prints abruptly left the road and started up the dry wash. Without hesitation I followed suit, making ready to drop my pack and gear in an effort to chase him down if need be. Yet after some fifty feet his prints looped back around and returned to the road, taking off again for Glenn Spring. I breathed an inner sigh of relief and did the same.

Northwards I plodded on, drawing nearer to water with each step I took. Every once in a while I would have to stop and take a breather. I didn't dare sit down or even squat; just stand there a moment, shift my pack, and lean into the harness again. Once past the draw I knew the road angled upward until the final half mile or so before dropping again into Glenn Spring. Mentally I steeled myself for this final ascent and kept pushing forward, aiming for that summit where I could coast in downhill from there.

Those needed breathers were coming more frequently as the sun beat down upon both me and that sorry, nameless flat. There was no breeze, no shade, nor any semblance of a cloud to provide the barest sort of temporary relief. I could feel my blood pumping as my heart forced the thickened fluid to my extremities, and could hear the dull thud in my inner ears as it worked doubly hard to compensate for the lack of body fluids. I was starting to really hurt and knew that I was becoming weaker.

For some distance I had been studying a steep rise of ground to my direct front. Even from afar, one could see some sort of man-made cleft surmounting the incline and I remember thinking, hoping, it wasn't the road. As I drew closer my spirits lowered as I saw that indeed it was, and I was going to have to follow it up to the summit.

According to the topographical maps for this area, that uppermost point did not even constitute two hundred feet as far as an elevation change. But from where I stood on that fiercely hot day and how I felt at that moment, it might as well have been two thousand feet straight up. I took one more short break, standing hands on knees in the middle of Black Gap Road, and began trudging up the incline.

All of the physical and environmental factors I had encountered so far seemed to combine forces as I did so, creating an ill-disposed foe which tried to push me back every step I took. What had begun as a challenge had become a struggle and now was an obstacle that acted as if it lived and breathed malevolence, trying to force me down and into the barren ground. My legs shook and my chest heaved, and I realized I wasn't sweating as much as I had before. It was yet another sign of my deteriorating condition.

The unrelenting sun beat down upon me; it was like being in a furnace with the thermostat set on high and no way out. About halfway up I stopped again and looked back on the dry, desolate land from where we had come. Absolutely nothing stirred; there was no sign of the slightest breeze to cool me. I was hot, thirsty, well-baked, and wrung out, and just about as spent as I could ever recall. Swaying on my feet I looked to the sky and mumbled something like "Lord, I'm not asking for a big miracle like the parting of a sea or a trumpet blast to bring down the walls of a city. But I sure could use a little breeze to help get me to the top of this thing."

Sighing, I grudgingly recommitted myself to the task at hand and started moving again. I had not taken more than five steps when I heard it coming across the flat behind me, rustling the branches of the stunted mesquite and wizened greasewood. It hit at just the right angle and I mentally caught my second wind as the cooling breeze propelled me forward. Upward and onward I went, and within a few minutes I had reached the top and was heading downhill to Glenn Spring.

As I did so the breeze abruptly stopped. Don't ask me how or why it happened that way, other than there is a God and He does look after fools, drunks, and the occasional wayward traveler reduced to heartfelt prayer. I am certain there are those who would scoff at such a suggestion, saying that someone else's idea of an Almighty has never made His presence known to them in any such fashion. You can think what you want, but I know what happened to me on that blistering early afternoon with my back to the proverbial wall, and it wasn't the first time.

About a quarter of a mile from Glenn Spring I could see Joe Gehrz heading my direction, a full canteen of water clutched in his hand. I thanked him with a mouth full of cotton and drank the contents greedily; it was the sweetest, wettest, most life-giving sensation anyone can ever imagine experiencing. Together we

Joe Gehrz, David Flannery, and Levi English at Glenn Spring

made our way to the bottom of the gulley which Glenn Spring runs through. Levi and David were waiting for us there, utterly drained and resting in the paltry shade of an overhang on the south side of the arroyo.

I went over to them and dropped my pack and gear while Joe found a spot for himself. No one said too much at first; we were too busy taking in moisture any way we could by drinking the fresh water of our cache, and dousing ourselves in the scantest of shallow streams emanating from the spring itself.

Joe began scooping up the brackish water from the stream and rubbing it into his short cropped blonde hair. He stared hard at the tiny rill oozing through the mud and half joked; "I feel like lying in it and flopping around like a hooked fish."

"Too late," replied Levi evenly, "I already have." He pointed to the area where the road crossed the stream in the arroyo, the sand and gravel bed disturbed by a recent flurry. His stained, discolored clothing told the rest of the story.

As the precious moisture revived us, we started comparing notes. Joe and David had made it in walking side by side, followed shortly by Levi, who did not bother to go any further than the rivulet itself; he just got down on his belly and drank his fill before rolling around in it. After taking a well-deserved rest Joe and David arrived back with our cache, and Levi filled a canteen with good water, intending to climb out of the steep arroyo and meet me. He hadn't taken many steps before realizing he wasn't getting to the top unless he rested some more. That was how Joe ended up bringing me the canteen.

Levi was somewhat emotional about this, saying that he kept hearing me call for help but couldn't get up enough strength to come my way. Joe said on the way to Glenn Spring he thought he had heard the sound of a bugle call, and David stated he was certain he heard horses in the distance. For those of you who know the history of Glenn Spring and what happened there, you might better appreciate the significance of those last two comments in light of the fact that neither of these young men were aware of its violent past.

I asked Levi about his boot tracks leading up the dry wash before returning to Black Gap Road. He said that he could actually *see* water in the draw a short distance away and instinctively started toward it. The mirage seemed quite real until he recalled my admonitions about not leaving the track, and why. At that point reality set back in, the illusion melted away, and he returned to the crossing and went on.

In the course of cussing and discussing the earlier events of the day, our talk turned to what should be done next. We were still some fifteen miles from the Basin and our vehicles, and the route was mostly uphill, with nearly a 4500-foot elevation change along the way. The idea of finishing our planned trip in our present physical condition was unanimously rejected by all hands.

After mulling over the available options we decided our best course was to flag down a vehicle coming off the river through Glenn Spring. One of us could hitch a ride back to the Basin, get one of our vehicles, and come back for the rest of us. Of course that depended on someone passing through who would stop, but I figured there would be some traffic later in the afternoon, as Glenn Spring sits at the junction of two roads that see some use. If this idea failed, we would stay the night, and two of us would head for the Basin at first light sans packs but with double rations of water. Until then our battered little expedition would rest up and wait.

And rest we did, in between drinking more water. I can distinctly recall David Flannery snoring peacefully face down in the creek bottom, small flecks of gray shale gravel blowing to and fro around his face as he breathed in and out. If ever there was a picture of utter exhaustion, it was him in that position. He was still at it when I heard a vehicle coming up Black Gap Road, which meant it would cross the creek not forty yards away.

"Boys," I said in a conversational tone, "here comes that ride we were talking about."

David's response was instantaneous; his head jerked skyward from his deep sleep and he came up at a dead run, moving up the creek and toward the crossing. His unshaven face was covered with granules of shale gravel and his disheveled hair was standing on end as he went. On visual impression alone I expected to hear the vehicle accelerating rapidly past and away from this wild man who had appeared from out of nowhere, in the middle of nowhere.

But the vehicle did stop, and as a matter of fact the occupants were heading toward the Basin. David rapidly explained our situation and arranged for Levi and Joe to ride along to pick up our vehicles. They loaded up with our startled benefactors and were on their way in short order, while David and I lazed around a bit more before gathering everyone's packs and staging them beside the road.

Sometime later Levi showed up with my pickup truck. We stowed our gear and equipment, and after joining up with Joe at the highway we were headed back to Ozona. The four of us spent the next few days not doing much more than drinking all sorts of liquids and just lying around recovering from our ordeal. I was still passing an ugly shade of brown urine about the color of that Glenn Spring mud when my compatriots boarded the airplane at San Antonio and flew back to Annapolis.

In all my years and journeys I can never recall coming so close, nor do I ever want to come that close again. There will be some reading these lines who will critique our efforts, saying they would have done this or not done that. A word of advice: unless you have been in the same situation facing the same difficulties, don't. A short time later, an illegal immigrant died along this same route, while several others with him were hospitalized.

That does not mean there were not lessons to be learned or blessings to be counted. Upon personal reflection, I couldn't have asked for better men to share this memorable trip with. Through it all not one complained, not one lost his head, and everyone involved continually pulled together as a team. One must have hard-won experience in facing tough situations to realize how rare and special this is in any group of men. I was honored to be with them.

Finally, there is one other matter which bears mentioning in this story. One day some weeks later a letter arrived in my post office box. Opening it, I found a simple card which read as follows:

Mr. English,

*That was the most fun I ever had
in a near death experience.*

Thank you!

Joe Gehrz

And when next spring rolled around, they all came back for more.

CHAPTER 3

In The Solitario

May you live all the days of your life.

—JONATHAN SWIFT

"I think we got a tire going down."

Those words are definitely something no one ever likes to hear, even in the best of circumstances. But when you are at the end of the line after some forty-two miles of dirt road, not to mention being over fifty miles from the nearest repair shop; they can be downright depressing. At least it had waited until we had arrived at our new campsite.

We were in the eastern part of the Solitario Mountains, which is one of the more desolate spots to be found in the Big Bend country. Our camp for the next four days would be at the *Tres Papalotes* (Tex-Mex for "Three Windmills"); the furthest camp from pavement in this over-three-hundred-thousand-acre slice of West Texas known as Big Bend Ranch State Park. The "we" consisted of a party of seven; five midshipmen from the Naval Academy at Annapolis who were full of youth and vigor, and Roy Glenn Sutton and me, who were way past the youth part, anyway.

Crawling out of the truck we confirmed what had already been suspected: the tire was going down, and that Chevrolet three-quarter ton was already taking a list to the starboard side. Armed with the knowledge that the lower a tire gets, the more jacking and grunting is involved, we moved fast and were tightening the lug nuts on the spare as the second group showed up in my wife's Dodge Durango. I think they were smirking a bit.

Yet youth and vigor does come in handy when setting up a campsite, especially when those in possession of such qualities are experienced hands at that sort of thing. In no time at all the tents were set up, gear was stowed, and everything else that needed doing was taken care of. As the sun began to set, the titillating aromas of supper cooking came wafting through our new domicile. There is nothing quite like grub prepared over an open campfire to help one rediscover his appetite, and the meal that followed was as good as it gets. You had to eat fast, however, otherwise you were going to miss out on any available seconds. An air wing of starving turkey buzzards could take lessons from this fast-eating crew.

During the interlude I made my habitual quick scout around the immediate area, getting my mind set as to what lay in relation to everything else. The Tres Papalotes is situated in the northeastern part of The Solitario proper, about a mile and half below what is called the Lefthand Shutup. It encompasses an old line camp which dates back nearly a half century before, to the time when this was private ranch land. The shack still stands along with one of the windmills the campsite was named after. This location makes for a natural base of operations if you plan to explore the eastern side of The Solitario, and that was precisely what we were here to do.

Since childhood The Solitario had been an ongoing mystery to me. The word *solitario* itself roughly translates into descriptors such as "seclusive, lonesome, solitary or desolate," and each one in turn fits that country to a tee. Back then our ranch headquarters sat just east of these mountains, with Lajitas to the south of them and our leased property holdings at Fresno Canyon situated along the western side of the range. I spent a lot of hours looking at those roughhewn peaks from three different directions and wondering about what might be found in between. Even the very appearance of the range can be fearsome. From some angles you can look across and see those flatiron ridges reaching up like the fingers of an impossibly enormous monster, trying to claw its way out from underneath a mountain-covered tomb.

There were also the stories; colorful tales about The Solitario which arrayed themselves against the common or everyday and acted as a high-octane fuel for my young imagination. My father had scouted the eastern side of this remote range many times by horseback and told me of things that he had seen and found

Flatirons on western side of The Solitario

which led to pure fascination on my part. He described it as a place where you never knew what you would see next, no matter how odd or bizarre it might seem considering the location. Several times he said that he would take me there someday, but that day just never came around on the calendar for me.

In addition to what he told me about The Solitario were the other stories I heard at the trading post in Lajitas, fantastic stories which had been passed down from generation to generation, along with a few most likely made up on the spot for the occasion. Some said the mountains formed a near-impenetrable circle around what lay inside, accessed by only one or two deep gorges guarded by hostile spirits. Others talked of riches beyond measure in precious metals found either naturally in the ground or carried into its confines by lost Spaniards, Apache Indians, or marauding bandits, depending on who was telling the story and when.

Furthermore, there was the talk about seeing strange lights in the sky, or luminescent orbs dancing from peak to peak across the range itself. Grown men would talk in whispers concerning certain locations when the arrow of a compass would wander about as if no longer sure where magnetic north actually lay. It was said to be a place best avoided, a rumored swallower of men

Vertical Strata in The Solitario

who had ventured within and never came back. Nary a sign of any of them was ever found again, save for an occasional eerie apparition that prowled about on the blackest of nights. As mentioned before, it provided the perfect stuff for a young boy's overactive imagination.

The decades went by, but I never lost my curiosity about those mountains, telling myself that one day I would go and take a look for myself. When offered the opportunity I would probe around their edges, often being left with still more questions than answers. The trouble was that not much was known about The Solitario, and the knowledge available was sometimes as questionable as the stories I had heard around Lajitas. Yet along the way I managed to cull some facts from the great amount of folklore and fiction concerning them. Ironically enough, what I discovered were several kernels of truth in the fanciful tales I had heard as a wide-eyed kid.

The most puzzling aspect of The Solitario was the geological influences which created this true anomaly of nature. Its outer reaches make for a near perfect circle that frames a large bowl in the center of this range, some five miles across at the widest point. It gives a first impression of being the crater for some huge ancient volcano or perhaps the impact point of an errant meteorite, but geologists say that it is actually the decayed remains of a laccolith. A *laccolith* is briefly defined as a dome of intruding magma between two layers of rock strata, causing a bulge between the layers. Once the magna cools it begins to decay relatively quickly compared to the rocks above and below. This particular laccolith has been slowly eroding away ever since, eventually leaving a massive cavity that can be seen with the naked eye from over a thousand miles in space.

The end result makes for an amazingly confusing geological Rubik's Cube yet to be fully unlocked or explained. Adding to this chaotic assemblage of rock formations and strata from assorted eras of our planet's history are some of the last visible remnants of the ancient Ouachita Mountains. Some 250 million years ago, these mountains were birthed when the South American tectonic plate pushed north against our own. In effect, the laccolith that formed the present-day Solitario blew up underneath the far older Ouachita mountain range, which once stretched from Chihuahua all the way into modern Oklahoma and Arkansas.

Such a tumultuous birth led to other geophysical complications, which helped explain some of the stories I had heard those many years before. There is a certain amount of iron ore deposited in these mountains, which accounts for the occasional weird swing of a compass needle. There are also precious metals in the ground underneath, or at least many a miner thought so. Much of the human activity that has occurred in The Solitario had to do with mining explorations. Numerous diggings for this purpose can be found along the eastern side of the bowl; counted among them were operations to extract magnesium, gold, and even uranium.

Yet there are more than just one or two ways into this isolated mountain range. In reality there are several points of entry, some of which can be iffy unless you have the necessary physical stamina and the knowledge to go along with it. Among these sorts of passages is the one called the Lower Shutup, which is a superbly steep-walled canyon that narrows at points to mere feet along its route. This twisting, jagged chasm goes on for miles and acts as the southern watershed funnel for a good portion of the interior of The Solitario. The route is difficult enough to force you out of the canyon at one point, and you have to know where that point is and which way to climb out. The Lower Shutup, along with the Lefthand Shutup and the opposing Righthand Shutup, form three of the more dramatic natural entrances into this basin.

By far the easiest way, though, is a high-clearance primitive track which winds its way from the north where it intersects the main road for the park. Once a mining road for the abandoned excavations found in the basin's interior, this is the accepted method these days of getting inside by vehicle. There is also a severely dilapidated jeep trail that climbs out of the southeast corner of the basin and weaves its way toward Black Mesa and the mines below there. Finally there is the now mostly forgotten Telephone Trail, one of the first man-made routes to pass through the range's interior more than a hundred years ago. Other, lesser-known approaches complete this list and serve as notice to the oft-repeated falsehood of there being only one or two ways into the middle of The Solitario.

As for those restless spirits of both the lost and the damned, along with whatever extraterrestrials might be lurking about; *quien sabes*? Again, there are kernels of truth to be found in most of the stories I heard as a child about these mountains. What with all of the other surreal elements linked to this unnatural creation of nature, I can think of few better locations to come across un- usual phenomena associated with the paranormal. It is just that kind of a place, especially after the sun goes down.

The next morning dawned bright and clear, and found us prep- ping for our day hike into the Lefthand Shutup. After a breakfast of eggs over easy and fried potatoes along with large helpings of refried beans, we topped off our water canteens and started out. Our main force was headed toward the easterly exit out of the basin, but Roy Glenn and my older son Levi decided instead to climb a nearby mountain looming to our southeast. Actually it was more like Levi deciding to climb the mountain and conning Roy Glenn into going with him. More on that little escapade later.

The rest of us launched north and began following a creek bed that soon became the canyon that formed the Lefthand Shutup. Multicolored rock walls rose on each side of us, topped by the clear blue sky—a visual impression not to be forgotten. By and large it was easy walking, other than the gravel and sand beneath our feet being so soft in some stretches that it tended to bog a man down. Those of us who knew the best way to traverse this sort of terrain showed the others how to pick their way along the firmer parts of the creek bottom.

In the Lefthand Shutup of The Solitario

It is usually dry in the Big Bend, and this March was drier than most. A warmer than usual winter with precious little moisture made for an early spring worthy of the word *desert*. Every step we took stirred up a little dust, and soon our boots and the lower parts of our trousers were showing the results. Yet as we trudged on, each became aware of the special kind of beauty that encapsulated us here. Perhaps it is more than mere coincidence the ancient prophets of the Bible went into the desert wilderness to make their inquires of an Almighty God. The overlying starkness of this imposing landscape provides a canvas that only He could create and then fill so fully; a work of art filling the mortal soul with contemplation and awe.

Within a couple of hours our leisurely pace had brought us to our destination, the spot where the Lefthand Shutup breaks out of the mountains and into the lower country below. Just short of our goal we discovered a small dam across the chasm standing about twenty feet high and filled in with silt. It was of a rock and mortar construction and had evidently been there for a long time, as it was beginning to crumble away on one side. Something seemed vaguely familiar to me in some of this, and it pricked half-dreamily at my consciousness, though I was certain I had never been here before.

As I surveyed the scene my mind abruptly began spinning in reverse to nearly a half century before, back to when my family had the Fulcher Ranch situated south of Hen Egg Mountain. Some of the adjoining property we leased crowded close to the east side of The Solitario, and in those days my father prowled a lot of this country on horseback. In an epiphanic flash my memory went to a small dam he described to me after finding it during one of his solitary rides. I had forgotten the story, but upon seeing this it all came back: this was the dam he had told me about. I found myself wondering what it must have looked like all those years ago. He said there had been small trees then, even including a palm, and some water.

When one's memories are sparked by a long-ago event, other recollections tend to follow closely behind. So I knew that somewhere downstream nearby was an old Indian camp. Going to the high ground beyond the dam I took a long look around and tried to recall those long-ago conversations from the time-induced fog enveloping a little boy's memories.

On another one of those trips, my youngest brother Barry had ridden with my father into this same area. He was only about five years old at that time, and during their ride described coming upon a boulder-studded rise of ground that was literally covered with hundreds of arrowheads in varying sizes and designs. Seizing the unexpected opportunity, Barry had jumped off his horse and begun filling his pockets with them. When my father saw what he was doing he had gently admonished him, telling my brother to leave them where they were. He explained they would come back together someday with someone who fully understood such things and could properly excavate the site. They never went back.

I scanned the terrain with my binoculars. About four hundred yards away was a low-lying bluff where the dry wash took an abrupt jog to the north. Something inside me said that was most likely the site of the Indian camp Dad and my little brother had talked about those decades before. I could discern the kind of ground features both had described, including that peculiar face of vertical rock. But there was something else that made my heart sink: a well-traveled dirt road running not more than a hundred yards away which formed a junction with yet another road. I knew then those arrowheads and whatever else was left of that camp had disappeared a long time before.

One side of me still wanted to go and take a closer look while the other cautioned against it. My topographical map showed that we were very close to the park boundary, and I did not want to stray onto someone else's private land, especially with a following group of aspiring military officers. So I did the next best thing by dropping into the creek bed again and getting as close as I dared, taking photos along the way. As I did so, I felt more certain than ever before this must be the place.

Nevertheless, an actual confirmation would have to wait for another day. I explained to Ethan about the dam and the possible camp so as to pass along my knowledge in case I never got a chance to return. We walked back to the dam and took our nooning there, eating and resting in the shade cast by the surrounding canyon walls. Once we had our fill we started the hike back, taking in the scenery from the opposite direction. There was an infinite variety of shapes, sizes, and composition of rock, including what appeared to be shelves of near vertical strata along our way.

About a half mile into the return trip Ethan, Nate Valaik, and Will Nutting decided to climb out of the crevice and blaze a trail straight across the rugged terrain. Their idea was to get more of a bird's eye view of what was around us before getting to camp. Both Nate and Will would become Marine Corps officers in the near future and were as solid as any two young men who had come with me to the Big Bend. After an impromptu briefing over a topographical map of the area, I cut them loose. Once they had managed to gain the high ground we lost sight of them almost immediately.

David Flannery and I kept to our prior track, and after meandering through the canyon arrived at the Tres Papalotes in good order. There we were greeted by the solitary figure of Roy Glenn, hunched up in a folding camp chair and nursing a recently shishkabobbed right thumb.

"What happened?" I asked.

He looked up at me, steel-grey eyes squinting hard against the mid-afternoon sun. At some seventy-three years young, Roy Glenn Sutton could match many a far younger man step for step in this high desert, and was as hardy and tough in nature as the wild country surrounding him.

"Aw, Levi and I were messing around on that mountain and I got some lechuguilla in the thumb."

Leaning over, I examined the damage. Lechuguilla is a tough, low-lying cactus with pointed splines on the end of its leaves. The tips are as sharp and hard as any mesquite thorn, and can be mildly poisonous. Roy Glenn had lost his balance on the rocky slope and one of those points, about half an inch long, had shoved itself underneath the thumbnail.

"Does it hurt?" I inquired half-facetiously. He gave me a look that would curdle fresh milk.

"Hell no," he retorted. "In fact you oughta try it for yourself; it builds character."

"No thanks, I've been one of those before."

"Do tell," Roy Glenn observed disgustedly.

"Think you got any poison in it?"

"Nah, Levi cleaned it out and we bled it good." He held the thumb up to better admire my older son's medical handiwork. "Then he doctored it for me."

Standing erect again, I took a long look around.

"Where is Levi, anyway?" I queried.

"Back over there someplace on some other mountain." Roy Glenn motioned his head towards the south. "He saw me to camp before heading out again. Said he'd be in before dark."

Dave and I sat down beside Roy Glenn and waited for the others to show up. A former Marine, Texas highway patrolman, border patrol agent, special agent for the Justice Department, and finally sheriff of Crockett County, my friend had lived an active life and often regaled the younger men with many a story of it. This afternoon was no exception, and soon enough Dave was on the edge of his seat listening to Roy Glenn spin his tales along with an occasional dirty joke.

"Tell Dave about your nickname in high school." I urged.

Roy Glenn kind of grinned on one side of his mouth and shook his head.

"What? What nickname?" David wanted to know as he sensed yet another good yarn.

"They used to call him 'Satan Sutton,'" I explained. "Something to do with riding a motorcycle through the main hallway when he was a senior, among several other deeds of local notoriety."

Dave guffawed.

"No, it's the truth," I insisted. "Last fall I had him come talk to one of my criminal justice classes about being a peace officer. One of his schoolmates said I needed to first check on the statute of limitations on some of the stuff he pulled before allowing him on campus, including the one about his motorcycle ride. Otherwise, he might be forced to arrest himself."

David guffawed again.

"Ain't that right, Satan?" I elbowed Roy Glenn good naturedly. The half grin on his face had now bloomed completely over, as a streak of bedevilment and a simple love of life danced merrily together in my friend's eyes.

"That was a long time ago, and I'm not admitting anything to you, Ben English," he growled. Then he leaned over conspiratorially to David and lowered his voice; "Still don't know what that statute of limitations might be."

About an hour later Ethan's group of three came waltzing in, no worse for the wear. Levi stayed out until after sunset, having scouted several mountains in the general vicinity of our camp. Each of us reported our findings to Ethan, who was acting as expedition coordinator, allowing him to figure where and how much distance each group had covered along with plotting the hikes for tomorrow. Total miles traveled for David and me calculated out at about ten miles, while Ethan and his bunch had gone a bit more because of the circling and climbing involved. Levi? Who knows, because he spent much of his day going almost straight up or straight down from one mountain to another. That night after a filling meal, we shared several stories that might have been partially true and turned in for the night.

The morning of day three was a bit warmer as we headed out to explore the area of The Solitario known as the Lower Shutup. As we made our way down the old mining road, you could see the magnesium diggings located to the east and nearly at the top of their mountain host. Ethan had set aside most of tomorrow's schedule for a special trip to those tunnels and to the remains of a uranium mine farther beyond.

Walking past the turnoffs to the inner and outer loops through The Solitario basin, we came to where the road ends and you drop into an adjoining creek bed. Nearby lay the signs of times long past: an old camp stove, rusting tin cans, hinges, and small pieces of mining equipment abandoned to the withering elements of the Chihuahuan Desert. One can only imagine the lost dreams and busted fortunes represented by these decaying castoffs, as well as the effort, money, and time that went into bringing them here. Men came and toiled and then went away, perhaps in pursuit of other dreams and other fortunes. The desert is a harsh mistress, albeit a patient one. Slowly, irreversibly, she was reclaiming her rightful territory and reasserting her authority over the grand schemes of both mice and men.

We moved on to the south, staying in the creek bed as the ensnaring grasp of the Lower Shutup funneled us in. If the Lefthand Shutup had been an interesting prelude to what was to come, then this canyon was proving to be the main event. The grade was steeper, the walls higher, and the passage often narrower as well as tougher to navigate. There were all sorts of rocks of every size and description, some better defined as boulders the size of large trucks that partially blocked and redirected the rough-and-tumble channel.

Many of these rocks, both massive and small, had been polished over the eons by the rushing water of flash floods cascading through. We came across solid sheets of stone lining the canyon floor that had been given the same treatment, and the rubber soles of our boots were hard-pressed to get a reassuring grip in some of these spots. The use of any kind of footwear with leather tread would have been like walking on greased glass.

Above us and to all sides were a myriad of color contrasts in the surrounding walls of the chasm, combined with the sparse green vegetation dotting the landscape and coronated by blue sky overhead. It made for a visual collage which provided an inner thrill for both the eye and soul of the beholder. Our little party continued on, dropping still lower into the canyon to the point where any breeze wandering in was stilled, and shade from the hot midday sun became a happy circumstance.

Finally we reached a place where the walls narrowed to the point of nearly closing, and the floor of the canyon fell down and away from us in a series of large boulders and water seeps. At the bottom of this obstacle-studded crag was a fairly large tinaja, which combined with the steep descent made going any farther a near impossibility without belaying rope. Getting back up would prove to be even more problematic than going down, and the jagged layers of unforgiving terrain running for miles in either direction looked formidable. I knew of the accepted way around this jumbled bottleneck, but it involved climbing completely out of the canyon, and we were already beyond our allotted halfway point.

Faced with such competing constraints we elected to take our nooning, eat, and enjoy the view from the cooling shade. Follow-

Rock walls of the Lower Shutup

ing our meal Levi, Ethan, and Will scrambled up the steep opposing canyon face to some shallow caves situated about a hundred feet above us. After exploring the larger of the two and satiating their curiosity, the three made their way down and our group started back to the Tres Papalotes.

As we cleared the high walls at the top of the shutup, we used our binoculars to study a dilapidated jeep trail winding through the higher terrain along the southeastern portion of the basin. I had spotted it on the way down and had a particular interest in this track, as it is another one of those lesser-known ways into The Solitario mentioned earlier.

If I had my landmarks correct, this mostly abandoned route winds its way beyond the farthest reaches of The Solitario, forking at certain places along its path. One fork, which was the earliest part and more like a trail, loops its way back around to Chimney Rock, which is situated below the Lower Shutup. Another leads to an old mining settlement known as *La Escondida*, while a third works its way along the south side of Black Mesa before coming to an end near the long-defunct Marfa and Mariposa Mining Company.

It is my belief this road's main purpose was to bring supplies and equipment from the Fresno Canyon and Mariposa/Terlingua

Levi, Will, and Ethan climbing to caves in the Lower Shutup

areas to mining operations up here. There is no easy way into The Solitario when hauling freight, but during the era in question this approach would have been one of the two that were doable. We took the time to be certain of where the route entered the main wash for the Lower Shutup and made a note of it for future reference. Walking out the remnants of this bygone relic and its offshoots was another item on my "to do" list for a future trip, but presently we would have to content ourselves with what was in our more immediate vicinity.

About halfway back we detoured to the site of an old gold mine situated just to the east and above the creek bed. Scattering like a covey of quail, each of us approached and studied the site with a different perspective as we roamed about. The tunnels had been grated over or covered with a sort of chain link barrier, leaving us the only option of peering into the darkness and allowing our imaginations to move on from there.

Having several mechanical engineering students in our midst provided Roy Glenn and me with some entertainment. Rocks were dropped into the vertical shafts by some of our younger members and timed to determine how deep these holes might be. Then a spirited discussion broke out concerning the exact formula and the precise mental calculations needed to establish the distance. Roy Glenn and I voted it deep enough to require grating to keep some lunkhead from falling in, and left the finer points to those with a yen for the precise number of inches to "lunkhead impact."

After arguing about terminal velocities and such, we finished looking around the site and got back on the trail to the Tres Papalotes. It was still some distance away, the mid-afternoon hours were slipping by, and necessary chores awaited us at base camp. Tomorrow was going to be another day of prowling about, and a hot meal along with a good night's sleep helps set a favorable tone for whatever might come.

The next morning found us with the most challenging goals so far: the explorations of the magnesium mine and the uranium diggings situated to our south. Both of these locations sat high on their respective mountains, which meant there would be a climb to reach either one. Decaying dirt roads were available leading up to them, allowing us the choice of following these tracks or taking a more direct path straight across country. On this day we would end up doing both.

In addition to examining these two sites I had a more personal quest in mind: I wanted to find the remnants of an old wagon track referred to as the Telephone Trail. Maps from the very beginning of the twentieth century made note of this route, and it was once the only way through The Solitario from the booming Mariposa mines known then as Terlingua up toward the Marfa area. As time went by, the path disappeared first from area maps and then from the collective memories of most who lived in the lower Big Bend. My intent was to locate any traces of it still to be found, and make it a part of the knowledge and memories of those much younger than I. On this particular jaunt there would be five of us; David and Roy Glenn opted to hold down the fort at the Tres Papalotes.

Upon our arrival at the abandoned magnesium digs our little trip livened up almost immediately. Though a casual glance determined that the main tunnel and its feeders had been dynamited or otherwise filled in at some time in the past, the desert and the creatures who live there have a way of wasting nothing. In the close proximity of the old shaft we soon discovered ample evidence to prove this out.

I have written before of the large numbers of hardy lechuguilla which cover this rugged landscape. About the only animal which can exist on a steady diet of the tenacious plant is the *javelina,* or desert peccary, and about the only thing that can make a steady diet of the so-called "skunk pig" is a mountain lion. This particular part of the Big Bend has always been thick with all three, and a representative of the top of this specific food chain had reconstituted the demolished main entrance into a made-to-order lair.

A pungently foul scent filled the air around the site, emanating from four decaying javelina carcasses scattered about the shaft's mouth. Piles of cat scat lay nearby, and the opposite wall of the opening was covered with copious amounts of dried cougar urine. All of these offending odors combined to overpower one's sense of smell, and sent our eyes looking in every direction in case the master of the house was still lurking about. However, the droppings were fairly old, and the freshest kill was at least five days past; the big cat was probably out on one of its seventy-five or hundred-mile loops usually coinciding with the time of the full moon.

We scrambled about the area, a steeply inclined locale with plenty of shale and loose rock. Above the main shaft were three smaller ones that had also been blocked off, along with assorted bits and pieces of abandoned mining equipment. Having satisfied our curiosity here, our main party broke into two parts: my bunch would make use of the road leading to the uranium mine, while the other group elected to take a cross-country route between the two points.

The uranium site is situated nearly due south of the magnesium digs, and a little over a half mile away when measured by compass heading. If you stay on the road, the distance is substantially farther. The main shaft for the mine itself sits roughly seventy-five feet below the very tip of the next mountain ridge over, its mouth covered with thick timbers and then sealed off with the same type of steel netting found at the gold mine the day before. As best we could estimate this vertical tunnel, fed by two large ventilation pipes spaced at lower elevations, was by far the deepest of the three mines our team investigated.

We took our lunch break here, munching on trail mix and power bars while scouring our collection of maps and comparing them to the terrain below. Our vantage point allowed us to see ground features not otherwise visible, including the remains of primitive roads from several decades ago that could be observed drifting off in different directions. With pencil and map these were plotted as closely as possible for future reconnoitering and research. No matter how basic, routes of travel do not exist in this country except for some express purpose, especially during the time period these evidently dated back to.

Somewhere out there were other spots touched by man, though probably not as grand in vision or as easily identifiable as the excavation site we rested upon now. They were also not on any map that I knew of, which meant that something of true interest might wait undisturbed along their routes. Though we did not have the time to discover their possible secrets on this trip, another foray on another day just might find the leavings of someone else's long forsaken fancy.

Finishing our lunch break we saddled up again to get the most out of the remaining hours we had in this day. Still keeping to two separate groups, Levi and Will decided to stay to the high ground, while Nate, Ethan, and I set out for a valley situated on the western side of the Blue Range. Our intent now was to find something of the Telephone Trail. While at the uranium site, I had identified some map features that might assist us in this search. Using the numerous crisscrossing javelina and mule deer trails available, we made our way down the mountain.

The Telephone Trail that once ran through The Solitario is not to be confused with Telephone Canyon, located in the easternmost part of the Big Bend National Park, nor with the path that leads there. The trail we were searching for is appreciably older than the one on federal land and dates back to the very dawn of the twentieth century.

Most people are not aware of the fact, but the first telephones came to this region much earlier than one might suspect. The reason for this unlikely circumstance was the existence of the mines. Cinnabar production was a fiercely competitive business in those decades, and the men who had the latest information on scheduling, pricing, and demand were the same ones who became millionaires while others went bankrupt or into receivership. Knowledge is power in any era, and in the years when it took better than a week for a load of cinnabar ore to make it from the Mariposa mines to Marfa, such knowledge was a tremendous advantage to those who possessed it.

A freight road had been laid out from the Mariposa (also called Terlingua for a short period) to Marfa before the turn of the century. Marfa was where the railroad was, which made it instrumental in the shipping of the ore. The route dropped off the Sierra de Cal and ran roughly west from that point along the base of the high ground until it intersected Fresno Canyon near Wax Factory Laccolith. From there the road traveled up the canyon for some miles before it topped out and headed for San Jacinto Mountain before attaching itself to Alamito Creek. From there north the road mostly paced this creek until reaching its final destination.

Most of this same basic route is still in use today for one purpose or the other, and is intrinsic to the history of the Big Bend of 125 years ago. It was nearly a hundred miles in length, and in its heyday as a freight road was ponderously slow in the best of circumstances. To alleviate this long delay in communications a modern marvel from the era was utilized offering instantaneous contact with the outside world, and that was how the Telephone Trail came into being.

Once the plans were finalized for the line, an ambitious amount of wire and supporting poles were brought in to run it from the Mariposa to Marfa. Yet even such a prosperous commercial enterprise as the Mariposa had to stick to a budget, and this advanced technology came with a steep price tag. It was decided that rather than having the phone line follow the roundabout freight road, it would take a more direct route through the northern part of the Solitario Basin. This cut the total distance down to about seventy-five miles. A service way for the placement, care, and upkeep of the wire followed along the line's path, and this track became known as the Telephone Trail.

Ironically enough the mine had pretty much played out by 1910, and the post office and accompanying name of Terlingua were moved about ten miles away to its current location at the then-competing Chisos Mining Company. The Chisos mines used the railhead at Alpine for their business, even running their own phone line to Alpine some years later. The one to Marfa from the Mariposa quickly fell into disuse, and the line itself simply vanished. Like I said, that technology came with a steep price tag, and the material needed for it was most likely salvaged for other projects.

Yet the service right-of-way remained. Over the next hundred years most of it has gone the same way as the line, but I reasoned there were still bits and pieces to be found if one knew where to look. I wanted to take that look, because it was not only a piece of nearly-forgotten technological history for this region of Texas, but also because the Telephone Trail was one of the earliest man-made routes to actually go completely through The Solitario.

Once in the valley, at a spot we had selected from our vantage point above, we found assorted proofs of some long-ago land ownership: fence lines much older than the nearby mines ran in ninety-degree angles to each other. In these were old gaps for the movement of livestock from one pasture to another, or for wheeled vehicles. The construction of the fences and their evident age spoke of a past from several generations prior, a place where fence posts with overhead bracing laced by barbed wire now slowly rusted and rotted away.

Within this small valley were multiple fingers of higher ground scarred and divided by erosion, which in turn formed small draws and dry runs interspaced with isolated copses of ground yucca and other assorted cacti. These individual runs and bottoms fed into a ravine running off to the north, the general direction of our camp. Across the way we spied a flattened area that perhaps was the site for some sort of dwelling or line shack at one time. Other than the site itself and the eroding fence lines, no mark of man could be found. If the Telephone Trail had ever crossed through here, all visible evidence of it had long since been erased.

A bit disappointed in this but still game, we picked another spot above the valley to survey this stretch of land from a different angle. Carefully studying the area we had just climbed out of, we detected the faintest marks of another trail farther to the northeast. It evidently ran parallel with the creek bed beyond where the ravine passed through a cut, and closely matched our 1903 map detailing the elusive Telephone Trail.

It was another slipping, sliding, scrambling descent from the ridge we stood upon into the lower area below. After reaching our chosen spot, we began following the obfuscated traces of an archaic wagon road which crossed the creek bed time and again. In another twenty-five years, it is unlikely that anything will be left of this part of the route, save for some mention of it on a yellowing page or map legend. Yet for the here and now it still gave physical proof that it had existed, and had mattered in the affairs of those men who once traveled it.

We followed the phantom-like track until we were north of our camp and certain that its traces ran true enough to erase any lingering doubts of authenticity. Finally satisfied, we left it and

(Left to right) Nate Valaik, Ben H., David Flannery, Ethan English, Roy Glenn Sutton, Will Nutting, Levi English

proceeded through a low saddle in the direction of home base. Along the way, Ethan explored another partially obscured road and some diggings on the side of a hill we had spotted earlier that morning. After finding large amounts of other big cat droppings around its entrance, he decided to keep his distance and return to the Tres Papalotes.

As the sun dipped low over the western reaches of The Solitario, we sat in camp and nursed our sore and abused feet, our cuts and scrapes, and sated our thirst while we talked over the events of the day. We had seen a lot, made some discoveries, and had sketched out plans for a future return. A filling supper was cooked over the campfire, and one by one we drifted off to our sleeping bags to spend our last night away from civilization. There we pondered more on what we had found until a sound sleep quickly came upon us.

Loading up the next morning I took mental inventory of what had transpired over the past few days, and what I had learned not only about this secluded land but also of those I had shared my experiences with. It is said that you will learn more about another man in five days of backcountry living than in five years of knowing him someplace else. I find no fault with that logic and felt blessed in having spent my time with these six other men who ranged in years from barely twenty to over seventy. Other than the differences in chronological age, each was very much alike in what counts in a man, and each would do to ride any river with, or to share any desert camp.

Life is made up of the recollection of memories, hopefully more good ones than bad. There were memories made in that far-flung area of The Solitario, and I carried away nothing but good ones.

CHAPTER 4

Land of Broken Dreams

*We look back upon our life only as on a thing
of broken pieces, because our misses and failures
are always the first to strike us, and outweigh in
our imagination what we have done and attained.*

—GEOTHE

The Big Bend is truly one of the crown jewels of the Lone Star
State, yet there are so many Texans who have never been there.
Those who do go usually take a drive along the River Road or
through the National Park or spend an hour or so in the Basin,
thinking those are the only worthwhile sights to see in this rugged, charismatic land. Nothing could be farther from the truth.

During the wandering years of my youth I traveled to over thirty different countries on four continents, and sailed upon many
a blue-water sea. Among those opposing points on the compass
are places I would like to see again, maybe even pass a little more
time enjoying them. But I only have one favorite where I would
choose to spend all the remaining years of my life, and where I
somehow always feel at peace, a place where I know I belong. I
have spent over a half century of my life traveling the Big Bend
in one manner or another, often enough on foot. Each time I go
into the backcountry, I come back with something precious to
put away in my memories. I am not near finished seeing it all.

It was the latest part of winter in an area of the national park
where I wanted to do some research for my second and third
novels. My base of operations would be a primitive campsite at
the mouth of Ernst Canyon, which also houses a well-known water source known as Ernst Tinaja. In old journals and documents,
it is also sometimes referred to as the "Big Tinaja."

A *tinaja* is a natural waterhole, usually carved into the rock

Chisos Mountains

canyon floors by the rampaging waters of flash floods. They, along with the occasional desert spring, are literally the life's blood of this dry and unforgiving land. As is said about gold, water here is often where you find it. It is also just as precious as the yellow ore, and many would argue more so. After all, you don't need gold to survive in the Big Bend, but you certainly need water.

Both the canyon and the tinaja are named after Max Ernst. One cannot talk much about this part of the Big Bend without elaborating on who this man was and what he accomplished. Max A. Ernst was a German immigrant of the late nineteenth century who first came to this area in 1898. He was a man of no mean ability and courage, and he came here in search of his future, settling in what was then known as Boquillas, Texas. This was not the only Boquillas on the north side of the river; the name would be alternated back and forth with another settlement that sat near where the Rio Grande Village campground is now situated. The particular Boquillas Ernst decided to settle in was also known as *La Noria*.

In the ten years following, Max Ernst proved himself to be a dynamo of human energy and entrepreneurship. Well-liked and respected by area locals of all ethnic strains, he quickly attained public offices such as county commissioner, postmaster, notary, and justice of the peace. Beyond that he was also the proprietor of a mercantile known as the Big Tinaja store, after the "big tinaja" nearby which would later share his name. Max Ernst was a true flesh-and-blood incarnation of the American Dream, and a known success in the wearing of his many hats until fate stepped in and events took a tragic turn.

On September 27, 1908, he was returning from the Boquillas, Mexico, area following an investigation into some forged documents. Riding alone on horseback to his home, Ernst had dismounted to open a gate near a sharp curve in the road when he was ambushed by a concealed rifleman. A single .44 caliber bullet fired by the unknown assassin struck him in the back and exited out his stomach, leaving a ghastly wound with protruding intestines. Yet the tough German was still able to remount his horse and make his way to a friend's place some two miles away.

Mortally gutshot, Ernst lingered on for two days before he died. There was a lengthy investigation into the crime, but no one ever answered for his murder. The location where he was shot can be seen just south of the tunnel leading to Rio Grande Village; in fact, the reason this later tunnel was built was to bypass the sharp curve. After Ernst's murder the spot became known as Dead Man's Gulch, a name that has since faded into obscurity. There are other, better-known locations, however, that still bear his name, including Ernst Valley, Ernst Basin, Ernst Canyon, and of course, Ernst Tinaja; all tributes to a man fit to match this weathered, faraway country he chose as his new homeland.

The rock-strewn floor of Ernst Canyon has many tinajas scattered throughout its nearly mile-long length, but none are as big or as deep as the one named after him. It is said that Ernst Tinaja is particularly treacherous when the weather conditions are abnormally dry, causing thirsty animals to fall into it while trying to get to the low-lying water. Trapped by its slick, nearly vertical walls; they ultimately suffer a slow, torturous demise by drowning. Only the desert could make a death snare out of such a life-giving resource; it is an environment that does not suffer the foolish or the unwary, be they man or beast.

The most popular way to approach the tinaja is by walking up the canyon. To get there by vehicle you turn off the highway going to Rio Grande Village and head up the Old Ore Road for about four and a half miles. This road is only recommended for high-clearance vehicles, and the northern portion of it can be a real handful no matter what the weather. There are several camp-sites along this route, including the one I was using at the bottom end of the canyon along with two more at La Noria itself.

Driving along about a half mile south of the turnoff to Ernst Canyon, you are likely to spot the grave of a certain Juan De Leon. He was a young ranch hand from the Boquillas, Mexico area, and much like Max Ernst was shot from ambush while on horseback. The killing occurred on July 19, 1932, but it was several days before anyone found the body. De Leon was buried close to where he fell because of the advanced decomposition of his body from the high heat, which is why his final resting place sits right alongside the road. Once again, no one was ever brought to justice for the murder. Unsolved homicides have been a frequent occurrence in the Big Bend for as long as so-called civilized man has been here, and there have been many more of them than what any official record will admit to.

After settling into base camp at the mouth of Ernst Canyon, my first hike was to La Noria. This forlorn site, which once bustled with activity and promise, is now little more than a greasewood-studded empty space along the eastern side of Tornillo Creek. The Tornillo is much like Terlingua Creek in that numerous ruins and abandoned communities dot their banks, especially along the lower reaches of both. But out of all the settlements along the Tornillo, La Noria was by far the largest and most populated.

Over a hundred years ago *La Noria* (Mexican dialect for "The Water Wheel" or "The Well") was a thriving locale, partially due to Max Ernst's Big Tinaja Trading Post. These days hardly anything is left save for some scattered rock foundations, pieces of rusting metal, and the remains of old firing pits left during the Army's stay. One of the soldiers stationed here with the Fourteenth Cavalry fell victim to the deadly clutches of Ernst Tinaja in August of 1913.

Following the passing of Max Ernst, the post office and name of Boquillas, Texas, were transferred over to the small community located where Rio Grande Village stands today. The spot known as "La Noria" appeared on the maps again, populated by both Anglos and Mexicans as well as several different units of the United States Army during the years of the Great Mexican Revolution.

Among these elements were those of the Third Battalion, Tenth Pennsylvania Infantry Regiment. Originally a National Guard outfit that had served with some distinction during the Civil War, it was still made up of many a young lad from the Keystone State who had never been west of the Mississippi. They arrived at La Noria in the scorching month of July 1916, and their unit diaries clearly show that their initiation to life in the Big Bend was truly an unforgettable experience.

The "Third of the Tenth" was there to relieve the Fourth Texas Infantry, which had been rushed to the La Noria area following the Villista attack on Glenn Spring some two months prior. When the Fourth Texas packed up and left, however, they also managed to leave with much of the equipment and personal gear belonging to their Yankee counterparts. This unfortunate situation was ultimately straightened out after some spirited discussion and was officially attributed to the Texas boys having "made a mistake." Still, Third Battalion learned to keep an eagle eye on their belongings from that point forward, no matter what the uniform any stranger might be wearing.

The attack on Glenn Spring, about twelve miles away, as well as on other nearby areas had everyone on edge, and the Third did their share of patrolling the vicinity. They also assisted with the growing refugee crisis as Mexican nationals of all types and ages spilled across the border to escape the twin catastrophes of revolution and famine that had enshrouded their tormented nation. These missions and the attending environmental difficulties involved called for a steep learning curve on Third Battalion's part.

Two companies of the men were stationed at La Noria and billeted in military tents. Their day-to-day camp life often proved to be as much an adversary as anything else they came into contact with. Supplies were sporadic, coming by truck from Marathon over eighty miles away along the primitive Old Ore Road. Oftentimes allotted rations did not arrive, and the troops were forced to buy what they could from the locals, culminating in one ill-advised case of obtaining several young goats without being properly versed in the preparation of the strong-smelling *cabrito*. After that particular incident, some of the native Pennsylvanians solemnly swore that they would rather starve than eat cabrito again.

The infantrymen also learned to deal with the scorpions, the rattlesnakes, the heat, the dust, and the bad water. While nominally carrying out their assigned duties, they also spent considerable time working on disabled Packard supply trucks headed for Boquillas or Glenn Spring, not to mention laboring to keep the makeshift roads in some sort of repair. It was hard, monotonous work that never seemed to end—but they were always up to the challenge. After all, those trucks coming from the railhead at Marathon were not only their supply line but also their contact with the outside world.

Within a few months Third Battalion received orders to turn their area of operations over to yet another army unit, this time a cavalry detachment better suited for the task at hand. The Third had to undergo one more ordeal, however, as a proper send-off from this harsh land and its hardy people. A few days before their transfer, their bivouac area was hit by what unit records described as a "tornado." Between the punishing wind and torrential flooding, most of their camp, situated where the wide wash from Ernst Canyon dumps into Tornillo Creek, was destroyed. No one was seriously injured, but once again the men lost much of their equipment and personal belongings. It was officially noted that when it came time to take their leave of this particular tour of duty, no tears were shed at the parting.

As I moved through what was left of La Noria, these little historical footnotes of a mostly forgotten place kept coming back to me. Knowing that most of the army units stationed here had set up either in or along that same dry creek bed south of La Noria proper, I made my way to a strip of nearby high ground for a better perspective. Sure enough, not even the passage of an entire century had erased the many signs of a sizeable encampment having been located here. I prowled about the area until the sun was low on the horizon, prompting me to beat a quick path back to my own camp for a hearty meal before turning in for the night. I was going to need plenty of rest for what was scheduled tomorrow.

When first light broke I was already up and getting my gear together. The goal for today was a hike to a long-abandoned ore tramway terminal which had been in use during the same decade that the Third of the Tenth was stationed at La Noria. Many people go there via a couple of well-defined trails coming up from the south along the Rio Grande Village highway. My plan was a bit different; I was going to approach the terminal from the north, while scouting about for some mining roads that had not been in use for at least eighty years.

But first I had to go over the Cuesta Carlota, a range of rough hills split haphazardly up the middle by Ernst Canyon. There are

Topside of Ernst Canyon

the remains of a road leading up to the summit of a low pass just south of the crevice, which in turn peters out into a trail winding down into the next valley over. Saddling up with my pack, I pointed my nose easterly and began the ascent.

Upon arrival at the top of the pass I was greeted with a desert view which was something to see. For the past hundred years the lowland below has been known as Ernst Basin, but in times before it was called the *Valverde*, or "Green Valley." The name itself gives a general idea of how it once appeared, though now it is best described as a dry, eroding flat running for several miles along a roughly north-south axis. Beyond the valley was a string of low-lying hills shadowing the foot of the Caballo Muerto mountains, while on the horizon the craggy peaks of the Sierra del Carmen jutted up from Old Mexico. If anyone wants to experience the essence of the lower Big Bend, this is a fairly good spot to do it from.

Yet I did not spend much time taking it all in; I had a long way to go along a route that hardly anyone attempts, to a location where I had never been before. I could relax and loaf a little bit on the way back, but first priority went to accomplishing what I had set out to do. The sun was shining and there was plenty of blue in the morning sky. It was going to be a good day.

Even with my pressing desire to get to the terminal, I did take the opportunity for a detour to the upper side of Ernst Canyon. Due to the numerous tinajas and layout of the canyon floor, sections of it were said to be almost impassable. I wanted to confirm that for myself, and besides, I had never been into the cut before from the upper entrance. If there was a relatively safe way through, it could make for a considerably shorter trip with far less up-and-down than when hiking over the pass. Additionally, there was my naturally strong disinclination to have only one way into or out of any given place.

Once in the canyon I found it defined by mostly vertical walls which narrow in places to a width measured in feet. As I made my way along the bottom, it became more difficult to negotiate. There were several tinajas of varying sizes and shapes along the route that had water in them. One was easily over six feet in length and appreciably deeper than it looked.

Not much farther down I came to a juncture which must have been the nigh-impassable part. Not that it actually was, but it could make for a tricky piece of business without some rope or a bit of luck. Since I was by myself and do not believe in dumb luck as a winning philosophy for staying healthy, it was time to turn around. Remember my "foolish and the unwary" comment from before? I began backtracking and resigned myself to using the pass for the next couple of days.

After making my way out of the crevice and into Ernst Basin, I took to some high ground and broke out my topographical map. It was an older general one for the area, but I figured it would suffice for my purpose. There I discovered the first snag in my grand undertaking: there was supposed to be an old wagon road running lengthwise through the basin. Except it wasn't there.

Let me rephrase that last sentence: the lower portion of this wagon road was not there *anymore*. When the ore tramway shut down around 1919, the route I was looking for quickly fell into disrepair as it was no longer being utilized. After a near century of being little more than a series of dashes on a map, the desert had pretty much reclaimed it as its own.

Never mind; I had a lensatic compass and I could still read a map. From my vantage point I could see the other route to the east, which once went to the tramway, coming around the backside of some foothills. Like many other roads of some antiquity, there was more than one way to get from Point A to Point B.

Such was the case here, and I quickly oriented myself by using the pieces of this road still visible and picking out some of the more prominent natural landmarks.

Within a few more minutes I was working my way toward a series of small canyons that fork away from the southern end of Ernst Basin, walking a zig-zagging course in hopes of finding something of that elusive wagon track I was seeking. Down the valley I went, occasionally detouring to gain some elevation for a better look at my surroundings. However, there was no sign or trace of it. This "road less traveled" was proving itself to be a bit of a phantom.

While walking along I glanced over my right shoulder and was startled by what would be best labeled as a rare optical illusion. Over the Cuesta Carlota I could see the top of Pummel Peak, which forms a part of the Chisos Mountains range. The peak is a prominent terrain feature and was most likely originally called "Pommel Peak" until some unknown cartographer misspelled the name during a mapping expedition. Nevertheless, what struck me at this moment was that Pummel (or Pommel) Peak appeared to be just the other side of the Cuesta Carlota hills, instead of its true distance of *nearly fifteen miles away.*

This fantastic sight stopped me in mid-stride, and my mind went into spin cycle as it processed logic and experience being contradicted by what my eyes were now seeing. The effect was so compelling that it bordered on disconcerting; I knew what the actual distance was after having seen those mountains from most every angle imaginable over the decades. Yet there it was, and I could see the detail of individual features on the peak as if they were no more than a couple of miles away. For a moment I was half expecting to hear the voice of Rod Serling welcoming me to *The Twilight Zone.*

Many have experienced this same phenomenon when viewing the moon low on the horizon, but I had never observed it to such an advanced degree, especially during daylight hours. The only clue the peak was actually that far away was the blueness of its appearance denoting the great span in between. The atmospheric conditions must have been just right, and I was the sole beneficiary of this unusual occurrence. Every few steps I would stop and look to the west over the Cuesta Carlota again, my mind still scrambling about in dealing with the conflicting sensory inputs from this rather peculiar event. Another two hundred more yards along my search pattern, and Pummel Peak could no longer be seen. Oddly enough, this would not be the only incident of this type during the trip.

Onward I went with no success whatsoever in finding the elusive road, ultimately coming upon the mouths of three small canyons near the basin's southern boundary. I was a bit hesitant to pick one and enter; time was running short and I had no intention of trying to make that pass after dark. These three different canyons were in fairly close proximity, and I did not need to make a mistake. The map was studied again and my back azimuth double-checked. Setting my jaw, I selected what had to be the right one.

As I headed into the cut, my eye caught an unnatural formation of rocks along the northern shoulder of it. Moving in closer confirmed my initial suspicion: I had finally found the sought-after ore route first used by wagons pulled by harnessed mules a century ago. A cursory study revealed that a great deal of work had been done to put a roadbed through this small canyon, and the remnants of those efforts still stood out clearly. In a celebratory mood, I took a long swig of water from a canteen and then leaned into my own harness. The road goes on forever and the party never ends.

Following the time-worn remains, I began finding metal bits and pieces from wagons and then later trucks driven by men now long dead and mostly forgotten. On the latest topographical maps, this decaying road is not even notated anymore. But during its prime it and the other track, which runs farther east, carried veritable fortunes in lead, silver, and zinc from the tramway terminal up to the railway in Marathon. It was the stuff dreams are made of.

Coming out of the cut, the road changed direction and started traveling roughly southeast across a large flat. Rising before me to the south stood the mighty vertical faces of the Sierra del Carmen, now much closer than they were when viewed from the saddle atop the Cuesta Carlota. To my east ran a barren, obstacle-strewn finger of this sierra, which intrudes across the Rio Grande and into Texas and helps shape the near thousand-foot drops in Boquillas Canyon. Known as the *Sierra del Caballo Muerto* (Dead Horse Mountains), these elevations are as inhospitable and desolate as any uplifted range that can be found in the Lone Star State. And they are aptly named, as those rock-studded

Ruins at the old ore terminal

ridges are fully capable of killing a horse or any other living creature, given half the chance.

The road dropped into a dry creek bed and vanished abruptly for a brief distance. When I came upon the traces again, they were far better defined as they joined up with the other branch of the route near the head of the canyon. Nearing my destination, I began to pick up the pace. From nearly a half mile away one could see upended timbers rising out of the ocotillo and greasewood. It was the terminal, or what was left of it.

In a decade closely paralleling the Great Mexican Revolution (1910-1920), ore of different types was carried across the river via a cable tramway that was replaced by a far longer, larger version around 1914. This terminal served as the northern end for this later system, being the turnaround point for a six-mile overhead tramway carrying buckets of ore from the Puerto Rico mine located southeast of Boquillas, Mexico. Those rotting timbers once formed a structure that stood three stories tall and towered above the surrounding landscape.

There is history to be found here, along with the lingering residues of immense fortunes made. Many know of the Villista raid against Glenn Spring on the night of Cinco de Mayo, 1916. Glenn Spring lies about thirteen miles almost due west from these ruins, and this attack is sometimes referred to as the last armed incursion into the continental United States by a foreign power. Four Americans were killed in that attack; three troopers of the Fourteenth Cavalry and the four-year-old son of a local storekeeper.

However, far fewer are aware that some four days later the terminal was also attacked by another band of Villistas. During this period it is estimated that hundreds of these "patriotic bandits" raided isolated locations scattered throughout the Big Bend area. At this particular spot eight employees of the International Mining Company, which owned the tramway, were captured by some of the roaming marauders. After being taken inside Mexico, the mine workers later escaped, bringing their would-be captors back across the river with them in a daring bit of tit for tat.

After World War One the tramway was closed down, most likely due to the dip in prices for precious metals. Looking south of the terminal one can still see the rusting tramway cables lying where they fell, leading off to the first collapsed tramway tower pointing the way toward Boquillas. At one time those cables and their supporting structures were responsible for moving seven and a half tons of ore per hour. The wooden towers were spaced at varying intervals dictated by terrain or elevation changes along the tramway's path. Owing to the high cost of salvaging the line, much of tramway was left in place when it was abandoned. The last time I checked, at least one of the towers was still standing.

After a quick late lunch of MREs and some more scouting about, I retraced my route along the road until exiting the mouth of the small canyon again. Coming upon the location where I had first found the unnatural line of rocks, I attempted to follow what remained of the track and was able to do so for a couple of hundred yards. But after that it just vanished into the basin again with not a remaining rut to be found. In a couple of more decades it won't be there at all.

When I reached the pass over the Cuesta Carlota on the return leg, I took my time going over the top to better appreciate the view. Nearing the summit my progress was halted by the unlikely sight of a pincushion cactus growing out of solid rock. Moving off the trail, I took a breather and marveled at this living definition of resiliency. To me it signified what it must have taken for those who lived here before man's technology managed to bend the will of this wild, seclusive land. After catching my wind I continued on, mindful of the many challenges each of us find in this world and how we respond to them.

Easing back into base camp around sundown, I made myself a supper fit for a king. Or at least, a famished and footsore wanderer who needed his strength for what lay ahead. As closely as I could determine from my topographical maps, I had managed to cover over fifteen miles on foot. The following day would prove to be every bit as long a haul.

Again I was up at dawn, fixing a full breakfast and double-checking my gear. Today I had scheduled a trip to the east side of Alto Relex, a large chunk of uplifted real estate some six miles due north. I wanted to explore the east side of this formation, including a canyon of some size running lengthwise against it. By the way, that was six miles as the crow flies; the actual distance would prove out to be substantially further.

Making my way over the pass for the Cuesta Carlota, and upon entering Ernst Basin, I turned north towards Alto Relex. There was supposed to be a trail leading that direction, and I picked up on the rock cairns almost immediately. I also picked up on something else: the tracks of another man in hiking shoes. Judging by them and his stride, this unknown gent was probably over six feet tall and somewhere around 190 pounds, and evidently looking around the area much the same as I was. His tracks were fairly fresh, too, possibly two but more than likely three days old.

Seeing human tracks coming and going from Ernst Tinaja itself is common; the tinaja is a well-known tourist spot and less than a mile walk round-trip from where you can park a vehicle. But out here? Whoever he was, he had to be a cat of a different breed than most, or someone who was doing their level best to get himself lost. As far as I could tell he had come in from one of the campsites in the Willow Tank area, walking in from the junction where the derelict ore terminal route joined with the Old Ore Road and then down into Ernst Basin. My own inquisitiveness was aroused, and I began following him.

He meandered back and forth across the basin itself, apparently just looking around and getting a feel for the terrain. Then he took to following the rock cairns marking the path towards the eastern reaches of Alto Relex. This path is shown on some maps as the Ernst Basin Trail and runs from the pass over the Cuesta

Carlota all the way up to Telephone Canyon Trail, some eight miles to the north. It also ran through the canyon corkscrewing along the eastern side of Alto Relex that I wanted to see.

The mysterious traveler made his way up the basin along the wide dry creek bed, which led to the entrance to that canyon. Some of the cairns marking the trail were either poorly situated or misplaced, and I could see where he became a bit confused and uncertain. Sometime later, we both ran out of cairns to follow. That is when he turned around, and I proceeded on.

I had hiked over to some higher ground on the far side of the creek bed to better see if there were any more rock cairns in the vicinity, and to just get a better lay of the land. While glassing the bottom end of my intended destination, I glanced to the west and was once again startled by the same optical illusion that I had been treated to the day before. Looming over some of the foothills between the Cuesta Carlota and Alto Relex was Pummel Peak again; appearing almost as if I could walk over that hill, reach out, and touch it. The bluish cast of its features still gave proof to the great distance, yet the details of the peak itself were appreciably sharper and more distinct than before. After spending a few more minutes studying the phenomenon and wondering just what forces were at work to create this rare event, I got back to my original objective and dropped into the dry wash again. There were other sights to take in, and I still had several miles in front of me.

On its northern end Ernst Basin narrows to a point marked by where the large creek bed first exits the environs of the unnamed canyon. The change in landscape contours bring part of the Dead Horse Mountains in closer for a better look. There is also a notable change in the native vegetation, the most obvious being the plentiful yuccas which can grow to a fairly good height. The tall plants make quite a visual impression among the other varieties of cacti intermingled with rocks and brushy undergrowth, all contrasted against blue sky. From the east several deeply cut gorges drain into the basin, making their way down from the Caballo Muerto range. In the future, I have plans to explore those numerous outlying chasms and ridges more fully.

From a distance the entrance to the canyon on the east side of Alto Relex does not look like much, but first impressions can be deceiving. Through it runs the funneling of a fairly large watershed extending all the way to the southern back slopes of

Canyon on east side of Alto Relex

Telephone Canyon. Past the canyon's mouth, the oversized dry wash gathers the runoff from western parts of the Dead Horse Mountains and channels itself through Ernst Tinaja and on to Tornillo Creek. Though rain is a rare gift to this parched land, you do not want to be in any of these canyons when it comes, especially those like the one where Ernst Tinaja is situated. One cannot fully appreciate the sheer intensity of the accompanying flash floods until you have experienced them for yourself. You can always hear the big ones coming; they rumble. That rumbling is from boulders being overturned by the unrelenting power of rushing water.

Once through the southern entrance, you come into close proximity with some of the sheer rock walls surrounding much of Alto Relex. When in the cut itself, you can often only perceive the first level of those precipices; there are others above and beyond your line of vision that are even more formidable. It is said that one can reach the top of Alto Relex by a relatively easy climb up the northern side or by angling in from the south tip. But from the east and west the ascent would range in classification from a "really tough challenge" to "you gotta be kidding me."

As I moved through the crevice, the staggered cliffs and walls began to form up on both sides, closing in all around. By now it had already been a several-mile hike from camp, and I was running negative numbers on my trusty Timex. But once in this gorge, I was mesmerized by the number of intriguing views in every direction. I kept walking farther into it and occasionally checking my watch, thinking to myself that I would give it just five minutes more before I turned back. From studying my maps, I knew that the top end of the canyon was not far away, and I wanted to see it.

And so it went for some time before I finally forced myself to stop and take a break. It was only then I realized it was my first time doing so since leaving camp. It felt good to take the load off my feet, and even better pulling my boots and socks off, wiggling my toes, and letting everything air out. The place I had picked for my quick nooning was at a large boulder ensconced in the bottom of the canyon, mostly flat across the top, which made for a Johnny-on-the-spot picnic table. I sat on the large rock looking all around me, enthralled by the surrounding panorama of colors, shapes, and angles. It was the sort of spot that seemed to mutate every five minutes with the passing of the sun, and visitors could stay fascinated with the scenery for as long as they chose to remain there.

Among the curiosities that caught my eye were the unmistakable signs of recent rockslides. Examining them, I idly debated with myself if any of this had to do with the earthquake that struck the Big Bend in April of 1995. It was reportedly the second-most powerful quake in recorded Texas history with an epicenter near Marathon, about sixty air miles north. It was also strong enough to cause part of the face of Cathedral Mountain, south of Alpine, to crumble away. There was one large chunk of rock in particular down canyon showing definite signs of recent displacement. It had fallen from one of the vertical walls in the crevice, leaving a vivid scar still unbleached by the sun or any other weathering marks. Time continued to slip past as I sat there in the solitude of the closed-in world around me. By now I was running way late, and it was still a long hike back to the campsite. Though I had wanted to make it completely through this canyon, it wasn't going to happen today. Reversing my direction, I scrambled in and around piles of boulders for a short distance before setting a ground-eating pace to where I had come from. As the canyon widened and my path became clearer of obstructions, I began recon shuffling my way along. There was no desire

Looking northwest from trail above Ernst Canyon

whatsoever in me to try that pass over the Cuesta Carlota on a moonless night, so I pushed on hard.

Nearly three hours of fast moving found me at the top of the saddle above Ernst Canyon, with the sun now hanging low in the western sky. It was where I finally stopped for a moment to catch a breath, soak in the scenery, and take some final photographs to serve as a reminder of this near-perfect day. From the pass you could see west and north across Tornillo Creek and all the way to the Chisos, back to the Rosillos, and all points in between. After taking my time appreciating these broad strokes made on the grandest of all canvases, it was down the home stretch and into my campsite again.

Once there I grabbed a folding chair out of the Durango and rested for a while before making supper. While taking this respite I also scoured my maps, making field notes and finally deciding I had covered over fifteen more miles on this day. My feet hurt and my legs ached, but I felt pretty good all in all. After eating supper and getting all of my camp chores done, I would feel even better.

That night I lay in my sleeping bag as the desert turned cold, thinking about all that I had seen on this trip. I also thought about those men and women who first came here, and what a fearsome opponent this land must have been to them. I felt privileged to be able to sift through some of the decaying ashes of their individual dreams, and also somewhat humbled. Those ruins at La Noria, the long-abandoned freight road through Ernst Basin, the ore tramway all gave mute testimony to those who braved a harsh and unforgiving land in pursuit of those dreams. Though some attained theirs and perhaps even more, most probably didn't. But they all tried.

And we in turn live in the shadow of those efforts, and can only marvel at what they did or attempted to do.

CHAPTER 5

Road Closed

*If you have men who will only come if they know there
is a good road, I don't want them. I want men
who will come if there is no road at all.*

—DAVID LIVINGSTONE

Sometimes things do not go as planned, and sometimes what comes out of such detours in life turns out to be even better than what had been hoped for. This trip turned out to be just such an occasion.

I was on one of my frequent sabbaticals into the Big Bend to finish out the research for a novel and just get away from civilization for a while. My exact destination was the Terlingua Abaja area, a couple of miles north of Santa Elena Canyon. I had been there numerous times before over the decades, and was planning use of one of the nearby primitive camping spots as a home base to work from.

For those with a curiosity concerning history, *Terlingua Abaja* was actually the first of three different settlements to bear the name of Terlingua. There have been many explanations of how that name was derived and the proper use of it. A popular claim states that it is a corrupted version of *Tres Lenguas*, or "three languages" in Spanish. This supposedly had to do with the different Indian tribes found along the banks of Terlingua Creek.

The creek itself, which runs past Terlingua Abaja and then dumps into the Rio Grande at the mouth of Santa Elena Canyon, was most likely called Terlingua before any community had the name. Yet even at that, this eighty-some-odd-mile-long natural causeway first entered official records as *Lates Lengua*. Like so many other names and places in the Big Bend, the origin is shrouded in some controversy because of the passage of time, lack of written record, and variances in individual recollections. If you ever want to try your hand at solving some enduring mysteries, have a go at digging into the how and why of all this.

What is known is that farming communities along the lower reaches of Terlingua Creek likely date back to the late 1700s, though each in turn was transitory. The main reason for this was the presence of two different nations of hostile Indians: the Mescalero Apache and the mighty marauding bands of the Comanche. Although they remained mortal enemies, both entities preferred to prey upon the simple peasant farmers and their ill-starred settlements. The booty to be had was far more plentiful, and any defending *soldados* were usually someplace else.

Much has been made of the Great Comanche War Trail and where its different branches crossed the *Rio Bravo del Norte* into Mexico. The three main crossings in the Big Bend area were originally located in the vicinity of San Vicente, Lajitas, and Presidio. Early on the Spanish attempted to blunt these bloody depredations by establishing nearby *presidios* at all three points. At best, these efforts were only faintly effective. The horseback buccaneers would either go around or simply barrel straight through, leaving utter devastation in their wake.

Truth be known, the Comanches went wherever and crossed whatever they pretty much pleased, using any route best suited for the particular time and purpose. There never was any human raider more fearless and daring than these nomadic predators of the Southwest. Unfortunately for the early settlers along the lower parts of Terlingua Creek, the combination of reliable water and available plunder made the mouth of Santa Elena Canyon a favored alternate crossing. Added to this was the presence of roving bands of outlaws, scalp hunters, and Comancheros who also feasted upon the easy prey personified by the mostly defenseless *peones* who tried to make a life in this merciless land.

The attacks would reach a level of viciousness and frequency where the inhabitants of these early settlements would simply abandon them, the survivors of the horrendous raids often never to return. On occasion, however, some of the more courageous did, joined by unbloodied newcomers who had not yet learned to fear the Comanche Moon. They would settle on a likely plot of land and soon enough, the cycle of increasing violence started again. And so it went until the Comanches were no more, followed shortly by their long-time blood enemies, the Mescalero Apaches.

In the waning decades of the nineteenth century one of those heretofore transitory settlements became permanent and was christened *Terlingua*. Like the others that came before it, the village was mainly a farming community making use of the rich, fertile soil found along the banks of Terlingua Creek.

When the cinnabar mining boom hit in the 1890s, a shantytown sprang up at the Mariposa mines, about ten miles to the northwest of the farming village. In turn, this boom-town encampment became known as Terlingua, and the area I would be exploring on this trip was renamed *Terlingua Abaja*. But wait with bated breath, because it gets more confusing. The present enclave and accompanying ghost town referred to as Terlingua these days is actually the third and final location for the *Terlingua* name. In fact, for many years some natives of this part of the Big Bend still referred to the third location as *Chisos*, after the Chisos Mining Company headquartered there during the first part of the twentieth century.

Not only has there been some head scratching and consternation over all that, but additional turmoil has occurred over the name of Terlingua Abaja itself, specifically the *Abaja* part. Some old-timers claim the settlement was originally called Terlingua *Abajo,* not Abaja. Furthermore, several Spanish language professors are on record as stating that using the term *Terlingua Abaja* would be grammatically incorrect.

Now while I have no doubt those original inhabitants could be quite right and the name was corrupted by some unknown cartographer or scribe, for the purposes of this missive I will continue to refer to the location as Terlingua Abaja. That was its name in my growing years and was used by both Anglos and many native Spanish speakers, whether grammatically correct or not. Perhaps it is wisest to say that Terlingua is best defined as "perpetual state of confusion," a long-running tradition that has managed to carry into the twenty-first century. When it comes to the history of the Big Bend country, such incertitude often marks the normal state of affairs.

In any event I showed up at park headquarters with a plan to encamp at Terlingua Abaja in order to explore it as well as other surrounding areas, coupled with a pressing need to be away from other people—all other people. Like other plans and needs falling under the jurisdiction of Murphy's Laws, neither of these goals survived first contact.

At Panther Junction a very nice lady park ranger informed me that Maverick Road, the lynchpin to these same plans, had been closed due to recent rains. With a million-dollar smile, she suggested I instead stay at the Cottonwood Campground and hike into Terlingua Abaja from the mouth of Santa Elena Canyon. She had many good words to say about this campground; it was nice, it was quiet, and I would like it. Plus, there was a decent chance Maverick Road would reopen tomorrow and I could move into one of the Terlingua Abaja sites at that time.

Someone once remarked that when it's the only ball game in town, you go get your glove. So I clambered back into my old Dodge three quarter ton nicknamed "Brute" and headed down the pavement, nearly forty miles of it. My first stop was literally at the end of the road: Santa Elena Canyon itself. It has been a lot of years since I first saw that dramatic cut from which the Rio Grande flows between two towering walls of stone, but I go again every time I am in the neighborhood. A word to my fellow travelers: If you say you have been to the Big Bend but you have never seen Santa Elena Canyon, then you have never been to the Big Bend. Mere words could never do it justice, so I won't even try. Just go; you can thank me later.

I left Brute in a secluded parking spot and began tramping around the vicinity, which also includes the mouth of Terlingua Creek. The sun was just above the canyon top as I finished up, and Brute and I travelled the seven miles back to the turnoff for Cottonwood Campground. Along the way I stopped and took some photographs of the surrounding terrain highlighted in the stark shades of a West Texas sunset. When I reached the campground I found it as described; it was nice and it was somewhat quiet, but I could already tell I was not going to like it much.

My first hint was the number of vehicles parked around; there must have been at least a dozen. They were mostly shiny new RVs and travel trailers, pulled by equally shiny new pickup trucks with special edition nameplates. The proper attire appeared to be sport shirts, sleeveless blouses, shorts of every color and description, and all manner of sandals and flip-flops. Most everyone present looked askance in my direction as Brute rumbled up, its mechanical-locker rear end making those distinct clicks as we turned into the entrance.

Santa Elena Canyon

Bailing out of the cab, I made ready for supper. The simple life: drop the tailgate, pull out my two-burner camp stove (a recently acquired luxury), and a skillet, and get down to the business at hand. The couple next to me was setting up a picnic table with all the trimmings, including wine glasses. That was the second hint that I was probably in the wrong place. It didn't help matters much when I ate my evening meal from that skillet with nothing but a spoon, and cleaned it out with some of my wife's famous homemade bread. Yes, Virginia, the barbarians have arrived.

The next day I was up in the pre-dawn morning, getting ready for what was to come. I did a final check of my gear, got out that skillet again and set to frying bacon with red potatoes and a couple of fresh eggs over easy. I happened to glance over at one of my forced neighbors, sitting there mentally devouring my meal with a pair of piteous eyes. His better half had him eating some kind of bran oatmeal mush out of a large bowl. The poor fellow had the distinct appearance of a condemned prisoner desperately looking for a path of escape.

With Brute's massive V10 shaking the windows and any near-by wine glasses, we made our way toward my debarkation point near Santa Elena Canyon. Along the route I stumbled across a pair of LEO-type park rangers. We visited for a few minutes and

I asked them when Maverick Road would be open again. I got a very noncommittal "maybe tomorrow" in return. This would be a common refrain for the rest of my stay here.

Launching from the closed gate across the entry to Maverick Road, I followed the dirt track for a few hundred yards before dropping into Terlingua Creek. A bit of elaboration here, if you will. Terlingua Creek is not your garden-variety small gully most people imagine upon hearing the words. In some places it can be nearly a half mile wide, flowing through different channels at different times to pass along floodwaters from downpours which can originate over fifty miles away. If there has been one thing that has given me a healthy respect for the power of a flash flood, it is this creek. I know it well.

But today was a beautiful day, and my first goal was to place myself somewhat south of where most consider Terlingua Abaja to be. I had prowled this area before, but always when pressed for time to get someplace else. I had felt there was more to be found in the vicinity than was revealed to the casual eye. A study of historical maps and papers during my book research supported that belief.

Making my way diagonally across the broad creek bed, I was pleasantly surprised by the amount of water present. There was more than I could ever recall before, and it wasn't dark, muddy, post floodwater either. It was clear and inviting, with bluish-green ponds running from one to another spaced along my path. The recent rains had also brought a sheen of green to the surrounding countryside, and it made me think of what this land might have looked like once, before the heavy hand of civilization had been laid upon it.

It is said that when the first farmers arrived, this creek was covered with a canopy of huge cottonwood trees and all manner of other flora. Wildlife abounded, and they even claim there was beaver in those days along the lower parts of the Terlingua. But antiquated farming techniques and general overuse of the land led to a calamitous end for this fragile ecosystem. The bleached, decaying trunks of cottonwoods long dead give evidence of this, as well as to the traumatic damage done by man when it is paired with the lingering drought that ultimately hastened the abandonment of the community.

On the western banks of the Terlingua the long lasting effects of this environmental damage became pronounced. What had first been a grassy flat and then fertile farm fields was now mostly a barren wasteland. with stands of twisted, gnarled mesquites scattered hither and yon separated by deep fissures of erosion. Occasional small clumps of native grass could be spied in spots, but all around this isolated greenery was nothing but dirt ground on which nothing grew. It was a sobering scene and a reminder of how vitally important good stewardship is of this earth that God saw fit to bless us with.

Once across Terlingua Creek I started coming upon ruins, lots of ruins a half mile south of what most people consider to be Terlingua Abaja. From higher ground one could discern the vanishing traces of irrigated farm fields that stretched out from these ruins, as well as the last fading marks of a wagon road leading to Sublett's Store, which was located along the river. I was seeing things I had never noticed before, and this alternative approach derived from the ashes of my original plan was already reaping unexpected rewards.

Working my way slowly north, I came upon the old cemetery for Terlingua Abaja. In actuality, there are two cemeteries located here, and some make the argument for three. A lonely, forlorn spot situated upon a low rise of pinkish-red ground, this is one of the most photographed locations in the area, and I took the opportunity to add a few more for my own collection. Standing among the graves marked by weathered wooden crosses, you can see the opening for *Bruja* or "Witch" Canyon to the west. This crevice chiseled into the midst of the eastern vertical walls of Anguila Mesa is the one point where you can conceivably climb up to the top of the mesa from this direction. I have been there before, and it would not be anything close to an easy ascent. Any safe attempt would call for a goodly amount of rope and associated canyoneering gear to get it done safely.

Beyond the cemetery is the other popular landmark in this long-deserted community, commonly known these days as "The Rock House." The intervening decades have not been kind to it, yet it remains more intact than any other dwelling in Terlingua Abaja. At one time this structure was the home for Joe and Sally Humphreys, and Mrs. Humphreys taught school here for years. After they left around 1919, the building became a full-time schoolhouse until it was closed down in the middle 1920s. Recently, other schools in the region have brought their students to this fallen-down relic to learn more of the history here, and

Graveyard at Terlingua Abaja

perhaps better appreciate the struggles of some for a basic education that so many others take so lightly.

After taking a short break and a couple more photographs, it was time to push on to the high ground lying to the near northwest. This boulder-strewn ridge made up of dark, volcanic rock is instrumental to the plot of one of my novels, and I wanted to put some boots down on the exact point I would be writing about. At the crest was a commanding view most every way you looked; one could see for miles and miles on most bearings.

While prowling about on top, I came upon a rather shy creature you do not often see during the midday. It was a black and silver rock squirrel, and he stood still just long enough for me to get some quick shots with my digital camera. The distance was too far, though, and I found myself wishing for my recently retired Canon AE1 with a good telescopic lens. As soon as I tried to move closer, the timid creature was gone in a flash.

Picking my way back down the loose rock that formed a small but steep arroyo, I slid to the bottom amid the thick undergrowth lining this side of Terlingua Creek. Crossing over it at a narrow part, I found myself yet once more enthralled with both the quantity and quality of the water contained in the run. There were portions of it that made me think of the Rio Grande itself during

Schoolhouse ruins at Terlingua Abaja

a dry spell. I truly felt blessed to see both the creek and the surrounding country with their best Sunday dress on, and tarried somewhat while soaking it all in. Someone once wrote a song with lyrics that went "If Heaven ain't a lot like Dixie. . . . " Well, I suppose I feel the same about the Big Bend.

It was still about an hour before my scheduled turnaround, and along the northern boundary of the park was an old ranch headquarters that I wanted to investigate the following day. So I started sizing up likely high ground to do some area reconnoitering by utilizing my map, compass, and binoculars. As time is always precious, I was also having one of my so-called "power lunches." That means I was eating Pop-Tarts and jerky washed down by canteen water as I walked along, trying to make the most of the hours remaining.

Off to my left and somewhat above, my eye caught a small runoff coming from a nearby hill showing the makings of a long-ago trail. I started to circle around, as it was a steep grade and there were easier places to climb that would better suit my purpose. But something compelled me to take that old runoff, so I put my canteen away and scrambled to the top.

It was there I found the graves: all four of them unmarked and apparently far older than any of those at the cemeteries in Terlingua Abaja. Standing on that cheerless hill, I tried to recall any mention I had ever heard or read about graves being here and I came up with a blank. Then I carefully consulted my maps, but I already knew what I would find: there were no indications of any burials whatsoever at these grid coordinates.

I examined the site in detail, looking around for any indicator of a marker or stone denoting who lay here or for how long. The graves had been positioned with some thought: three side-by- side along a north-south axis while the other was some yards away, angled along the route of the passing sun. All four were covered with an assortment of stones big and small, and one could not even tell which end of the grave was supposed to be the head or the foot. Beyond those rudimentary findings there was nothing, absolutely nothing, that could be discerned. It was an absolute mystery, and my mind whirled with questions popping up by the dozen and no answers whatsoever to help balance them out.

I made written notes of the exact location and took several photographs of the site, and later discussed the photos and grid coordinates with a park ranger acquaintance of mine, a man well versed in the history of this area including the various settlements found along Terlingua Creek. He had never heard of these graves either, nor could he give any explanation of why they might be there.

My acquaintance did pass along the information to a park employee who specializes in such things. As of this date, I still do not know the whole story about what I unwittingly came across. The park authorities are justifiably closemouthed about gravesites and items of archaeological importance, and for very good reason. Unfortunately, grave desecrations and outright theft have become more common in the park over recent years, and they are trying to do everything possible to protect what is left. This is especially so for sites that are basically unknown and thus unspoiled. In like mind and for the same reasons, I will only write in general of my discovery.

In a century where there are few real mysteries left, I lay no claim to being another Sir Aurel Stein finding one of the lost cities of the Taklamakan. I am also quite confident these graves have already been documented by others, perhaps in ways still to be discovered. Nevertheless, the episode left me with a mixed bag of feelings—perplexity for one, parrying with a sense of minor accomplishment. Just happening to stumble upon this site served as a reminder that one never knows what might lie over the next hill or around the next bend, especially in a place called the Big Bend.

Moving beyond and away from the hilltop burial ground, I picked out a more inviting locale and broke out the binoculars again. I was still looking for that ranch headquarters mentioned earlier. On my 1903 map it was listed as the Dryden Ranch, and its ruins are also notated on the most recent quadrangle version. To plot tomorrow's route to them, I needed to get a good fix in regard to how they lay. With the ruins positioned as they are along this particular stretch of the western side of Terlingua Creek, following a somewhat straight line through the heavy brush can be a real challenge in navigation. The intervening maze of creek thickets are chock-full of unforeseen impediments which bite, prod, poke, or sting those who blunder into them; some preselected landmarks to guide by makes this onerous task much easier.

Following a minute or so of map and compass work I managed to locate the site, a good mile across the creek as the crow flies. After visually scouting out a likely path to it, I turned south to return to my morning departure spot by a different way, hiking through the ragged line of hills which lie between Terlingua Abaja and Maverick Road. It was an interesting interlude through an area which can be best described as otherworldly, the sort of terrain that would make a good backdrop for a science fiction movie. Dirt and rocks of every hue were mixed into an Indian blanket collage of contrasting colors. The land itself was divided, subdivided, and then laid bare by the intersecting arroyos and dry washes. These snake through the mostly denuded ground, occasionally adorned by a lonesome ocotillo or other desert plant.

As I cleared the southern edge of these barren hills and was traversing the head of a draw that ultimately dumps into the Terlingua, I managed to locate the last remains of yet another road that once ran between Terlingua Abaja and the old Sublett store and farm. This complex figured large in the early farming efforts in this area, and its ruins, along with the dwellings of other families such as the Dorgans, are still there, just off the north side of Ross Maxwell Highway as you drive toward Santa Elena Canyon.

I trailed the rutted route until it crossed Maverick Road and then angled my path cross-country to get back to the truck. It was late in the day when I climbed into Brute's cab and pointed the front bumper toward Cottonwood Campground. All said and done, I figured I'd covered about twelve miles on foot this day. It had been a pleasurable walk-around, but tomorrow would see the need to put on some speed.

The next morning was not as pretty as the first one; the vestiges of a front were moving through, accompanied by an unusually brisk breeze. But it was somewhat cooler and the change in weather could work to my advantage. After watering up and making certain my canteens were filled to the top, I started out on foot again from the same location as the day before.

This time I traveled due north, staying east of Terlingua Creek and taking a more direct aim for the Dryden Ranch ruins observed the afternoon prior. Along the way I came across several more ruins on this side of the creek, situated nearly a mile away from what might be termed "Terlingua Abaja proper." While in the area I even found the rusting frame and fenders of a Model T Ford, quietly wasting away beside the disintegrated shell of an adobe dwelling. No guess as to how long it had been there, but if there were stories to be told of forgotten roads and journeys of nearly a hundred years ago, one could find oneself wishing this discarded heap of scrap metal could talk.

Not too long afterward I was on yesterday's high ground studying the ranch headquarters from afar and figuring the best way to get below the bluffs dropping into the creek bottom. Swinging wide and picking up a faint game trail, I managed to make it to the bottom without any undue calamity or drama and pushed on.

In this particular part of Terlingua Creek there are several large stands of mature cottonwood trees, surviving reminders that give hint to what this area must have looked like all those years ago. The main creek bed through here is actually made up of three different channels paralleling each other, with the individual branches containing water at different points. In a land where watercourses are carved out by massive amounts of rushing water when infrequent rains come, varying channels are formed, utilized, and then bypassed by the tremendous force of these flash floods. This needs to be kept in mind when using topographical maps, since the older the map, the greater chance the creek channel displayed is not the one in use now. I crossed each one of the alternating runs in turn, adjusting my path to deal with the ponds and small thickets along the way.

The real obstacle before me was the same one I had observed from the bluffs the day before. On the west side of the creek was a dense thicket made up of stunted mesquite, cat claw, assorted cacti, and most anything else to constitute a near-impenetrable barrier at certain points. This brush line was almost one hundred feet in depth and long enough to preclude any easy detouring around.

Several times I had to fight my way through or go in a parallel direction, or back up completely and try a different approach. It reminded me of hot, dusty days spent as a kid in this same creek bed on the back of a half-broke horse, and why leggings were required equipment for such skin-shredding work. It is also not a good place for your mount to spook, either, and is why I learned to trust my own two feet far more than I ever did any horse, or mule for that matter.

But once through the thick brush I found I was only a few yards south of where I intended to be. My exit point was nearly perfect, as I could see the off-kilter markers belonging to a grave-yard on a low rise in front of me. Like many other settlements up and down Terlingua Creek, this ranch had included a cemetery. From where I had come out of the thicket, it was almost on a direct line to the headquarters itself.

Mindful of where I was and the significance of those assorted mounds of stone, I counted what I estimated to be eleven graves. I say estimated, as some of these unknown souls had been laid to rest on the eastern slope of this small knoll. Decades of rain and erosion had washed many of the covering rocks out of place or completely away, along with most of the wooden crosses. Later on I brought this up with park officials, who assured me they were keeping an eye on the site and would take whatever action necessary to stabilize it.

Moving northerly beyond the graveyard, I continued on to the ruins which once made up the Dryden Ranch headquarters. The ranch house itself must have been a rather large residence for this part of the country, constructed of part rock, part brick, and part adobe. Its sun-bleached bones also included the trunks of mature cottonwoods that had formed the rafters of the now-collapsed roof, giving yet more mute testimony to what these surroundings must have looked like over a century ago.

A little-known fact is the Dryden was not only a ranch; it also incorporated a sizeable farm as well as a brick-firing kiln. Many of the bricks found in other ruins throughout this area came from the Dryden furnace located near this spot. But like so many other

Dryden Ranch ruins

undertakings, it was ultimately abandoned to the desert realm from which it was created. The brick kiln operation was on the other side of Wells Creek, about a half mile away from the ranch headquarters. There are those who tend to combine the two as being solely at the headquarters location, but that was simply not the case.

An unusual set of artifacts found here are several tiny rock shelters neatly arranged just southwest of the ranch house. Constructed of the most common materials readily available, these individual structures were built upon the ground out of rock and scraps of wood. Enclosed on three sides, they each had an opening facing to the east, and the entire assemblage was surrounded by barbed wire to apparently secure what was kept inside.

The same style structures can be found around settlement ruins throughout the Big Bend and have been the subject of much speculation as to their purpose. As best I can determine, they were used to shelter and protect *cabritos*, or baby goats. These animals were a vital part in the life of the Anglo and especially Mexican-American pioneer families who came to this region, and every effort was made to make these family herds as abundant as possible. That fence was an attempt to keep predators out as much as it was to keep the baby goats in.

After spending some more time looking about the headquarters and sizing up its layout, I moved on again. My planned trek took me roughly west, along the northern boundary of the park. I was heading towards the *Sierra Aguja*, also known locally as Needle Peak. When my grandparents ran the Lajitas Trading Post, they kept a huge rock collection out back of the store for people to rummage through for possible purchase. Many of the more spectacular agates in those piles came from the Needle Peak range. The Sierra Aguja is mostly privately owned, but guided tours are available these days to rock hounds who desire to go there.

At times the park boundary parallels a near faded-away track which was the route from Dryden's Ranch past Coltrin's Camp and on to the Mariposa mines, about ten miles away. There is not much of this road left, and I could never recall being on it before, but the farther I skirted along it the more a vague feeling of *déjà vu* settled upon me. This notion became stronger as I approached the remains of a rock building near the foot of Sierra Aguja.

The surrounding landscape was eerily familiar to me, though I still could not put my finger on exactly why. Yet as I wandered about and gave it more thought the realization hit me: I actually had been here before. But it was nearly a half century past, and these crumbling ruins still resembled a habitable dwelling of sorts. I had come here with my grandfather, Bennie English, whom I was named after.

Giving it some more thought, I began to recall having being here more than once. Most always it was at night when picking up a load of candelilla wax, and my grandfather had let me tag along. He was good about that and very patient in this regard; I suppose he knew that he was teaching me valuable lessons which at the time I never realized I was learning. The reason I could not place this locale at first was because we had always approached from the Lajitas side, and thus from the opposite direction.

For a magical moment I let the decades slip away in my mind and I was seven again, following along in the large footsteps of a man who was like a superhero to me. A sixth generation Texan, he had lived the life of a man's man and is still one of the toughest men I have ever known. But most of all he had been my Papa and was instrumental in raising me to be who I am today, at least for many of the better parts.

I savored this memory for all it was worth before it receded into the mists of time and distance, to that personal Shangri La where precious memories are kept for all of us. It was time to take a breather, have a little lunch, and recollect some favorite thoughts of a man the likes of which they don't seem to make anymore.

There was also plenty of wondering to be done, too. I never knew how this old rock house got here or why, and I doubt there is anyone left alive who does. The pondering of one mystery often leads to another, and my mind turned to those four unmarked graves sitting upon that hill. It was an odd and lonely place to be laid to rest, but then again perhaps that was precisely the intention.

Who were they? How did they die? More importantly, how did they live? Was there anyone left on this earth who knew where they lay and would mourn for them? Could anyone even now recall their names or a single event from their entire existence?

As usual, a lot of questions with no answers, much like many of the other puzzles in life. I finished my meal, readjusted my pack harness, and pointed my face to the south. They say that much of what counts is in the journey itself, not just in the destination. *Quien sabes*? There were still sights to be seen on this particular trip, and I was burning daylight.

My next intention was to find some remains of yet another road that had run from Terlingua Abaja to Lajitas. This route was also the shortest way to get from the long-vacated farming community up to the Mariposa mines, which by this time had appropriated the name *Terlingua* for their own. The last record I had been able to find of this track dated back to the early 1930s, and antiquated maps showed that it had intersected the Dryden Ranch-Lajitas route near my present location. After a bit of reconnoitering I managed to find this road junction, but that wisp of a track soon faded into nothingness as it branched off to the south.

Settling upon an alternate path, I shifted farther west to walk the eastern foothills of the Sierra Aguja. If there was any remaining sign of the road, it could be more easily spotted from higher ground. Though unsuccessful in that regard I did enjoy the view, weaving my way along in this fashion for some distance before dropping back into the barren, eroded flats just northwest of Terlingua Abaja.

During the decades in which Terlingua Abaja was populated, many efforts were made to irrigate this stretch of flat land, all

Eroded flats northwest of Terlingua Abaja

with less than desirable results. Some of the efforts were quite ambitious; including what was described as a "tunnel" that was supposed to transfer water from a marsh near Terlingua Creek. Like other projects it ultimately collapsed, in this case quite literally. The ground proved to be too soft, and when flooded the tunnel simply caved in.

This soft soil, along with the cyclical flash flooding and the general overuse of what nature saw fit to bestow here, combined forces to bring about the results seen today. Erosion is a persistent problem, and its advancement has left scars upon this land which will take centuries to heal. Even after all the intervening years since man last farmed here, portions of the land still look like moonscape due to the great damage done.

When walking into the old settlement from the northwest, it is hard to believe there ever was marshland in this vicinity. As one gets closer, one can see the thick brush along the west bank of Terlingua Creek, giving only the slightest clue to what was once there. In stark contrast, the mostly bare flat where I now stood was mainly a series of crumbling washes, bare dirt, and near desolation. After nearly an eighty-year passage of time, only isolated clumps of grass are beginning to be seen again where acres of lush vegetation once grew.

Ruins below Terlingua Abaja proper

Coming through the low pass into Terlingua Abaja proper, I could finally see some evidence of the road I had been searching for. It wasn't much, but there was enough to show where it had run through the saddle and into the village. Trailing these remaining traces through the cut gives you a fresh perspective on the abandoned community, since you are coming at it from slightly above rather than approaching from the creek below. Because of the intervening terrain, a person can get fairly close to the old schoolhouse before actually seeing it. You walk around the slope of a hill and there it is, only about a hundred yards away.

Following my long-established routine I stopped there again, taking a breather and studying the lay of the land along with how the crumbling ruins around it were situated. What appears to the casual observer as relatively flat ground is anything but; the landscape is crisscrossed by a partially masked series of dry runs, small draws, and steep washouts feeding into the Terlingua. After taking a few more pictures, I scribbled down some pertinent notes and dropped into the creek bed for the final leg back to the truck.

Never being one to go back the same way I came if I can help it, I stayed in the main channel for a distance before angling toward the opposite bank. This proved to be a fortunate decision, as I spied a small flock of ducks bobbing peacefully in one of those ponds of blue water seen the day before. Even on the bare, stone-covered creek bed I was able to get fairly close before they thought me pressing enough to take wing and fly away. It was a sight you don't see every day in this country.

Continuing on I climbed out of the creek bed to the eastern side, walking along Maverick Road for a short distance before forking off toward the original overlook for Santa Elena Canyon. Decades ago this was a favored spot for taking photos of the imposing chasm. At one time you could drive to the tip of the ridge and park your vehicle at the overlook, but the entrance has been blocked off and bladed under for many years now.

After spending a few minutes to take in the view, I started working my way off the escarpment to where the truck was. I was about halfway down when I came across a large piece of a petrified tree trunk lying lengthways on the ground. Some two-and-a-half-feet long and nearly that wide, this fascinating example of nature's handiwork must have been sitting on that slope for the past several eons. It was yet another rare find, as well as a near-perfect finish to this day's walkabout.

The final morning I was up early at the Cottonwood Campground and making ready for a long drive back to Ozona. There would be no primitive campsites for me this time around; Maverick Road was still closed. Evidently it had rained much harder on the upper end of the route than had first been reported, and the park service was rightfully erring on the side of caution before letting anyone through. My original plan had come to naught.

No matter; I had come in search of what might be found and had gotten far more in return than I ever hoped for. You see, when one road closes there is usually another to be found just beyond where most of the herd will go. Yet if the journeyer will look for that other way and stand ready to take it, he will understand what is meant about the road taken to get there.

CHAPTER 6

Pilgrims in the Promised Land

This hill, though high, I covet to ascend;
The difficulty will not me offend,
For I perceive the way of life lies here:
Come, pluck up, heart; let's neither faint nor fear!

—JOHN BUNYAN, *THE PILGRIM'S PROGRESS*

It wasn't that I was lost; it was only that I couldn't seem to get where I wanted to be. My older son Levi and his crew had launched out the day before and were at a campsite along the upper reaches of the Fresno. Chris Johnson and I had come down the day following and were presently trying to figure out just where that camp might be.

Levi had told me it was right along the old military road near the top of Fresno Canyon. I recalled this route forked in the canyon floor near Post Mountain, with one track joining what is now called the Main Park Road about three miles east of the Sauceda. The other, which was the original way, snaked farther up the canyon and teed into that same park road less than a mile from The Solitario turnoff. Trouble was, I wasn't sure which one they had set up our camp on.

Aiding and abetting in this present quandary was the little matter of a missing map. Levi, now a freshly minted second lieutenant in the Marine Corps, had liberated it from my case and failed to make me aware of that pertinent fact. So when I asked Chris to get my map out, it was nowhere to be found. There's just something about second lieutenants and maps.

Panorama to the west from Fresno Peak

Things sort of snowballed from that point forward. I knew the camp wasn't far from whatever roadway it sat by, so we eased along, trying to spot some tents or Levi's battle-scarred GMC Suburban. We kept easing all the way to the turnoff for The Solitario without seeing anything. Reversing our direction, we now began the hunt in earnest.

We started by scouting the three Montoya campsites, where the original military road tops out of the Fresno. There was no sign of that other bunch to be found, so we backtracked to the western fork, which winds past Post Mountain. Stepping out of our Durango to check for tire tracks, I heard the unmistakable sound of air escaping from a Goodyear Wrangler on the right rear. Yep, it was going to be one of those days.

Yet all was not lost as I did manage to spot some tracks on the western fork that looked much like the Michelin all-terrain tires on Levi's GMC. Chris and I jumped back into the Dodge and headed down the smaller road, hoping the tire would hold up long enough to find them.

I looked over at my young friend and pastor, whose outsized frame seemed cramped even in the front seat of the large SUV. He was sitting there serenely with a jubilant grin on his face, which happened to be the usual state of affairs for him. At some six foot six and some change Brother Chris Johnson was a hard-muscled redwood tree of a man, and by physical appearance alone about as unlikely a Baptist preacher as one may find. That is, until you considered that special light which shone from within. I have known a lot of sky pilots in my time, and more than a few that I wouldn't give a bucket of warm spit for. Chris Johnson made up for all of those others and then some.

That right rear did last long enough, but just barely. We rolled into the La Posta campsite with very little air to spare and after unpacking the Durango, the flat was changed.. It was as good a time as any to remember that out in this country you only have what you were smart enough to bring along; any outside help is often far off and a long time coming. When traveling the back roads of the Big Bend there are basic essentials every vehicle should have to keep the party going: plenty of water, plenty of fuel, a shovel, a heavy duty can of fix a flat, and a good spare tire. Or better still, two good spare tires, if you have the room.

Once the tent was up and our gear stashed away, we sat down with the other three to catch up on the latest. Levi, my younger son Ethan, and Joe Gehrz had already been here for over a day, and had made good use of it by hiking the western fringes of The Solitario. It was spring break for all three of them; Levi and Joe had already graduated from Annapolis and were pursuing their master's degrees, while Ethan was still a midshipman at the Naval Academy. Along with Brother Chris, I couldn't ask for better men to share a campfire with.

I asked about their previous jaunt and heard how the trio had ventured down the old military road for some distance, hiking below the Righthand Shutup to the twin caves known as *Los Portales*. These caves are situated on the east side of Fresno Canyon and make for a fairly spectacular landmark, but very few visitors actually get to see them because of their somewhat remote location. Set into the near-vertical faces below the uppermost ridges of The Solitario, they look out from their perch hundreds of feet above the canyon floor. From some angles the site can appear as a crudely done rendering of a grinning Neanderthal man, with the large whitish boulders along the canyon floor serving as teeth that only a dentist could love. The twin caves are his eyes, and above the left one is a deep cleft marking a long-ago battle scar. The scraggly brush scattered about completes this stone caricature by forming an equally scraggly beard for him.

Los Portales

After climbing past the caves the three young men continued on, traversing the northern edges of what is known as the Flat Irons along the western side of The Solitario. Among these immense sloping ridges are massive slabs of sheer rock the size of oil tankers, jutting out along the outcroppings of this geologically stunning jigsaw puzzle. It is an amazing array which must be seen up close and in person to fully appreciate. Beyond this area the three of them ascended out of the canyon, then pushed on to within a half mile of the summit of Fresno Peak before returning to our new base camp at La Posta.

Their walkabout was a fair bit of gallivanting in anyone's book, and I listened with rapt attention, making notes for future reference. It had been many years since I had traveled through that section of the Fresno or The Solitario, and they had explored parts of both which I never had the opportunity to see. Their reports made me that much more anxious to get started doing so.

As the shadows grew long we cooked supper over an open campfire, then followed it up by telling stories and staring up at the night sky until time to turn in. The meal was filling, the heavens twinkled with the luminescence of an untold number of stars, and some of those stories might have even been true. Good thing we had a Baptist preacher with us.

At the crack of first light we were all moving about, shaking off the effects of the desert chill and making ready for a full day to come. The aroma of camp coffee drifted through, followed shortly by those of sizzling slabs of bacon, fried potatoes, and a host of eggs over easy. I have had a lot of breakfasts in my time, but for some reason those eaten in this fashion always seem to be the tastiest and most memorable.

We had decided the night before to strike out for The Solitario through the Righthand Shutup by way of the old military road. Levi felt certain we could drive as far as the point where the route begins to drop into Fresno Canyon, but was not sure whether we should try to go any farther. He wanted me to take a look at the descent once we arrived on location.

Our gear was loaded and soon enough we were standing at the spot he had spoken of. Together we walked down, studying the road to see if it would be feasible for our use. After examining the disused and rutted roadway as well as its abundant scatterings of loose rock, we decided to play it safe by launching out on foot from the escarpment above. I had no doubt we could take his modified Suburban down this particular stretch, but getting the heavy vehicle back up might be a different matter entirely.

So we saddled up and moved out, our starting point roughly north of Post Mountain. For those who might be trying to follow this journey on a topographical map, a few words of explanation are needed. For some unknown reason Texas Parks and Wildlife insists on using Mexican dialect for landmarks and locations that originally had Anglo names. In this case, Post Mountain is listed in all their literature as *La Posta*.

Now I have in my possession copies of area maps going back over 110 years, and every one refers to that particular peak as Post Mountain, not La Posta. Since I can read Mexican Spanish about as well as any other *Norteamericano,* this is of small consequence to me. But for others who can't, trying to correlate a USGS map with the park literature may provide for a certain amount of confusion. You don't need any confusion about landmarks in this kind of country, especially on public land where you have lots of newcomers wandering to and fro.

Once in the canyon bottom we came across the fork that connects with the original military track working its way north out of Fresno Canyon. This dilapidated, long-abandoned route from

Lajitas to Marfa has a great deal of local history and lore attached to it. Before the military adapted it to their use during the border troubles of the early twentieth century, these ruts carried millions of dollars' worth of cinnabar ore from the Mariposa mines west of present day Terlingua up to the railway in Marfa.

Some folks have recently started referring to it as "the stage road" because a stagecoach line once used it, but far more freight wagons were up and down this route than there ever were stagecoaches. In fact, if it hadn't had been for the freighting of mining ore and supplies there would have been no reason for a stagecoach line, or much of one for the road itself.

During the Pershing Expedition and the era of the *Gran Revolución Mexicana*, it served as a thoroughfare for a generation of young officers who would one day lead our nation to victory over the Axis Powers, including then-Second Lieutenant George S. Patton Jr. Closer to my own family roots, it was also how an underaged private traveled from Marfa to his new duty station in Lajitas. That was, until the Army found out he was barely sixteen years old and sent him back home to Winters, Texas. His name was Howell Coatis Cash, and he was my grandfather on my mother's side.

Following the end of the border troubles, the road still served as the main route from the Lajitas area up to Marfa through the 1930s and beyond World War II. When I was a small child it was called "the military road" by most of the locals, which is why I do the same. But no matter how one chooses to refer to it, if this threadbare, rock-strewn dirt track could talk, what tales it could tell.

And occasionally, physical evidence dating back thousands of years allow it to do so. About a half mile north from where the Righthand Shutup dumps into Fresno Creek is a large rock overhang, just off the east side of the roadway. Embedded in a small knoll above the creek bed, it makes for a fine place to observe any movement coming up or down the canyon. For as long as man has traveled through here, he has utilized this spot on account of the shade, nearby water sources, and tactically sound positioning. We climbed up to it, dropped our gear, and took a break from the sun.

Recently the park has started referring to this spot as *Manos Arriba*, Spanish for "Hands Up" or "Overhead." If one examines the southern portion of the natural ceiling formed by the overhang, the reason becomes obvious: there are numerous human handprints painted along here. Though varying in size and color, each one shows the wearing effects of time and weather, which speaks of their advanced age. Though there are many such spots to be found in the Big Bend, this is one of the few sites anyone has made public and advertised.

The covered area is fairly large, nearly ten feet from the overhang's lip in places. Much of the natural ceiling has been blackened by countless campfires, while a partial berm of soil and stone runs across its front, adding to the protection from the elements. Resting with the others, I idly wondered how many men had sought shelter here over the centuries, and for what reasons. Archaeologists say there has been human activity in Fresno Canyon for the past nine thousand years, and judging by what could be seen, I would wager that some of the earliest took place right where I now sat. It was a sobering thought, and brought to mind how short life is for any of us.

After a few minutes at the overhang we were back on the road again, still heading south. From here it was about half a mile to where the Righthand Shutup empties into Fresno Canyon. Within this same half mile there are also a couple of good-sized arroyos which snake in from the west, making for distinctive terrain features easily located on any map of the area.

For those interested, the two canyons to the west side contain the remains of a couple of trails: one leading beyond Old Log Spring, while the other eases past Seep Spring. Both ultimately ascend on top of the steep escarpment; the Seep Spring route toward the ruins at Howard's Ranch, while the Old Log Spring path continues on to the Sauceda. Though long unused for the most part, these trails followed natural runs and saddles, so by reading the right map you can figure them out fairly closely. A word of caution however; you need access to the right maps and possess the ability to read them, not just look at the lines. Otherwise you can get yourself and whoever is with you into a real jam.

There are also two ways through the Righthand Shutup to access the interior of The Solitario. On foot you can make your way straight up the canyon if you are willing to do some climbing. Riding an animal, a person can take an old trail which meanders north of the shutup before veering across the gorge and south for Burnt Camp. Not much is left of this route, because it ran along

Up the Righthand Shutup

several creek beds and cuts that have long since washed most of it away. But if you have a mind to and can get hold of the right map, you can follow the traces. This way is easier to navigate as far as the terrain goes, but it's definitely the long way around. Since we were on foot and ready for a challenge, we chose the shorter, more difficult path through the bottom of the shutup.

Our little group made this trip during one of the drier spells to hit this country in decades. Hiking up the canyon, we found that all the tinajas along the way were dry. The environs of The Solitario itself are notoriously arid by nature; there are no natural springs in it I am aware of. At one time there were working windmills and water tanks scattered around, but all of these have fallen into disrepair. The only other forms of water containment are a few small dams and dirt dikes built many years ago, the best known being McGuirk's Tanks. However, rain is required to fill them and there had not been any measureable amount for months. During our combined scouring of this mountain range, only one tinaja with water turned up, and it was not easy to find.

There are some fairly strenuous spots to navigate in the Right-hand Shutup, and a couple of near-vertical climbs at dry water-falls standing nearly twenty feet high. Yet none are insurmount-able, and moving up in elevation allows you to better plan where to next put a hand or a foot. As most experienced hikers will tell you, there can be a lot of dead space when you are moving from a higher altitude down to a lower point, especially in rugged terrain. Sometimes this unforeseen dead space can lead to problematic circumstances with no good solutions.

Though the ascent isn't easy, if a person wants to experience the essence of the harsh, stark beauty of The Solitario, this is a good way to do it. Someone once opined the Big Bend was where God left all the extra bits and pieces after creating the world. With that in mind, you can look upon The Solitario as His personal rock collection from those remains. This sixty some-odd square mile eroding laccolith is one big pile of rocks of every type, size, and description, often heaped upon each other haphazardly with no apparent rhyme or reason as to how they ever ended up juxtaposed in such positions.

In other stories I have written of how this range was formed, and the forces of nature that have acted upon it at different times and for different geological reasons. The canyons running through The Solitario act as ready incisions of an autopsy to expose what resulted within, and why. Like its counterparts the Lower Shutup and the Lefthand Shutup, the Righthand Shutup makes a deep, jagged cut across the staggered rims of these mountains, allowing the curious an opportunity to see this in exquisite detail. In effect, you become privy to the decaying bowels of what transpired here eons ago.

Onward we moved, taking in the shapes, colors, and design of all that was around us. Added into the mix of rocks of every shade and variety possible are the fossils; this land which is now high desert was once an inland sea trough. If you take only a second look, you will be amazed at the varieties of aquatic life exhibited in the surrounding stone; the effect is almost like a prehistoric gallery of undersea art. At one point we came across the fossilized remains of a fish in near perfect side relief, encased by a sheared brownish-colored rock, which in turn was framed by the large granite boulder displaying it. This is only a single example of many to be found in the area.

Slightly over two miles after leaving the Fresno we reached Burnt Camp Trail, which was originally an old wagon road. After taking a break for lunch we started back through the shutup. Some might think this a redundant effort, as we had just come from there. But in jumbled-up country like this, a turnaround

Petrified fish in boulder

affords the chance to see the same route from a brand new perspective. It is why you should study your back trail on occasion; it helps keep you oriented in such jagged, sometimes confusing terrain. Besides, the next accessible track was some distance over and would place us farther south than we had hours to allow for.

The Big Bend can be a precarious place to be, and the desert frames hard lessons why in the oddest of times and fashions. An incident underlining this fact was encountered on our way back, near the mouth of the crevice. I was pulling point for our group as we walked single file, boots whispering in the sand, when I heard movement coming up the canyon.

Freezing in place, I gave the hand and arm signals explaining such to those behind me, and faded into the low brush and shadows along the west side of the gorge. Quickly the others followed suit, led by my two sons. Some might think such a response to be a bit paranoid, but you just never know who or what you might run into out here. Whatever it proved to be, I fully intended to have the upper hand in the affair.

The sounds came closer. Whoever they were, they were either dog tired or were deliberately trying to kick over every loose stone to be found on that canyon floor. Soon enough I could hear voices; younger people, both male and female, speaking in an accent not native to this part of the world. Each one sounded bone weary and played out. We waited quietly, curious to see who it might be.

Rounding the next bend came five people: two young women paired with like males, trailed by an old man who looked ready to keel over face first. All of them appeared physically disheveled and beyond sunburnt, plodding along in the dreamlike pace of those who are having to concentrate on simply putting one foot in front of the other.

Too preoccupied with their combined miseries, they didn't see any of us until we stepped out into the open. Our sudden presence startled them, and I saw fear in their eyes as well as the instinctive urge to run, but they were just too spent to do anything other than stumble to a halt. The old man shuffled over and sat down heavily on a low ledge, not uttering a word. It didn't take much to realize this bunch was in sad shape.

As we began visiting with them, I studied each one in turn more closely. They had on shorts and sleeveless tops with little to nothing in the way of sun protection or suitable hiking equipment. One of the girls wore sandals and a halter top, and all were burnt by the sun to a deep, boiled-lobster shade of red. I noted that none of them had anything akin to water canteens, other than a single dime-store facsimile, along with a few water bottles.

Their tale of woe was a familiar one for those who come to this country unprepared and unaware of the challenges it can present. They had left their vehicle at the Burnt Camp Trailhead inside The Solitario, and on a lark decided to walk to Fresno Canyon and back. At this juncture they were still nearly three miles from the trailhead and their vehicle, and had no map, no food, no water, and little idea of where they were. In fact, they had run out of what little they had taken with them before even reaching Fresno Canyon.

We offered up some of our own water stores but they refused, saying they had found some not too long before. One of the young males described finding a small, stagnant waterhole in the bottom of Fresno Canyon that provided just enough to slake their building thirst. I cut my eye to Levi and Ethan who were standing close by, looking straight back at me. The three of us were thinking the same thing: with this long dry spell, there was no telling how long that water had been in that hole or what might have been swimming around in it.

Growing more concerned, we volunteered to get them to our base camp and then on to where they had left their vehicle. Where we stood now was roughly halfway between Levi's GMC and where they had parked, but it was a far easier hike to get to his Suburban. In the meantime, our party could act as a safety net in regard to their welfare.

Again, our offer was refused. They were determined to make it back through the shutup, and were adamant about not needing any help. Maybe it was because we had surprised them, or maybe we looked like a rough crowd, but I suspected they still had no idea just how precarious their situation might be.

I studied them over again. By all indications this crew was going to be in a real hurt locker in short order, and that old man was considerably worse off than his far-younger compatriots. I say old man: on closer examination he was likely ten years younger than me. But the desert had sapped him dry in more than one manner, and it showed plainly. Throughout our conversation he sat there and never said a word; shoulders drooped with a vacant look on his face. The scene made for a pitiful sight.

Levi, never being one to take *no* for an answer lightly, made another attempt at offering them water, and was once more rebuffed. He didn't like it much, and neither did we, but we had pushed the subject in polite terms about as far as it would go, and weren't about to argue with a bunch of total strangers when it came to their own best interests. Our party wished them well and they started shuffling up the canyon again, the old man dragging along in the rear. Joe Gehrz, our resident medical hand studying at Dartmouth, watched them leave and slowly shook his head; his blue eyes reflecting the disbelief and concern he felt inside. Oh well; God looks after fools, drunks, and pilgrims in the Promised Land. We turned our faces the opposite direction and went our own way.

However, the Good Lord wasn't through pulling overtime on this side of The Solitario just yet. We were about a mile up Fresno Canyon from the mouth of the Righthand Shutup when we heard a vehicle coming. This in itself was a fairly rare occurrence, but not totally unheard of, as the military road is still passable along this stretch to four-wheel-drive traffic. But imagine our combined consternation when a shiny new black Toyota Sienna drove past us in resplendent fashion, headed south toward the Smith Place.

Through the tinted windows I got a good look at the occupants. There was a younger man along with two little girls about eight to ten years old, evidently his daughters. He had rap music playing on the sound system and the air conditioning blowing full blast, slouched back in the driver's seat like he was cruising around the neighborhood on a Saturday afternoon. Again we got the distinct impression he was not from these parts and had no idea of the situation he had not only gotten himself into, but also those little girls.

"I think my Suburban just got punked by a minivan," muttered Levi under his breath, as the dust kicked up by the black Sienna settled around us.

"I don't see that Toyota back at the top of our hill yet," I commented, referring to where we had left his GMC. "Getting down it was the easy part."

"He had all-wheel drive," remarked Brother Chris, who had observed the callout badge on the rear hatch.

"Not the same as four-wheel drive," I replied, "and he also doesn't have enough ground clearance to get a real run at it."

We pushed on to get to the top of the hill. It was a steep incline; the elevation going up some three hundred feet in the space of a quarter of a mile. But what made it so treacherous for a vehicle were the multitudes of golfball- to fist-sized loose stones that littered the way up. In spots, hikers could lose their footing merely by walking along, if they weren't paying attention. Imagine the difficulties of a five-thousand-pound, off-road wannabe shod with passenger-car tires.

At the Suburban we took a few minutes for a breather and to admire the scenery from on high. Chris was trying to learn the country, so I took the time to point out some of the landmarks and how they sat in relation to what was beyond our eyesight. As we were stowing our gear in the GMC, the sound of the returning minivan drifted up the canyon. Levi had said the road was washed out below the Righthand Shutup, and apparently the driver of the black Sienna had not attempted to prove otherwise.

"Brother Chris," I announced, "I hear the main event approaching, and we have the best seats in the house." Grinning as always, Chris followed me over to a pile of large boulders overlooking the canyon. The other three did likewise and we perched up in those rocks like a bunch of turkey vultures, waiting on something to die.

The black Toyota traveled serenely up the dilapidated road

until it reached the bottom of the ascent. The driver got no further than about a hundred feet into his first try before the wheels started slipping and his forward progress ground to a halt. He eased the minivan into reverse and rolled back down for another attempt.

"Round one," someone said.

Still with a sense of decorum, the driver reached a spot to launch his second run. This time he made his approach at a faster pace, spurring the black minivan up the incline. But he hadn't gotten even halfway to the tough part before the Toyota dug in again; the spinning tires throwing up a cloud of fine dust that enshrouded its shiny black paint. Round two was also firmly decided against the Sienna.

By now it was dawning on this fine example of Darwinism that he had gotten himself into a real pickle. He couldn't retreat down the canyon because of the washout below, and the road was posted as impassable beyond the Smith Place. If he couldn't make the hill it was a long walk back to the Saucedo, or he might try for our camp since it was along the way. That is, if he had been paying enough attention to see the camp as he drove by. My bet was that he hadn't, and he also hadn't a clue as to where he was now or where he had been.

The driver managed to free the Toyota from where it had dug in and backed downhill again. He continued to roll past where he had come to a halt before, setting himself up for a final showdown between his new minivan and that obstinate piece of decaying road crawling up the west face of Fresno Canyon. In his madly racing mind, it was go-for-broke time.

"This is where it gets good," I told Chris.

The Toyota lunged forward, accelerating rapidly as the driver threw caution to the wind. He careened up the first part of the incline, barely maintaining control of the bouncing, rollicking minivan. It was already painfully obvious that things were not going to turn out well for that black Sienna.

Just past the point of his last attempt was a rise in that wasted skeleton of a road, a small levee placed years and years ago in an attempt to protect the surface from further erosion. Behind it was a large washout rutted lengthways on one side, hidden from his view by the mound formed for the levee. The Toyota bounded over the low rise, setting itself up perfectly for what was about to happen.

We didn't actually see what happened due to some intervening high ground. We didn't have to; our ears told us all we needed to know. There was a sickening reverberation as the minivan's underbelly collided with stone and caliche. The sound of the impact carried down the canyon as a large column of airborne dirt rose above the commotion, marked again by the racing of an engine and the spinning of tires. Only this time the Toyota wasn't going anyplace.

"Oops," someone breathed.

Wearily, Levi trudged over to his Suburban and dug out his shovel. Ethan and Joe joined him, getting out the crowbar and any other tools or equipment that might be of use. Together they started off the hill toward the black Toyota.

"Where you going?" I called after them.

"To see if we can get them unstuck," responded my older son.

"Not likely," said I, "unless you can put that thing on your back and carry it up. It's not going anyplace now. We'll probably have to go to the Saucedo and let the park people take care of it."

"Gotta try, Dad," he shouted over his shoulder.

"By all means, then." I gave them a flourish with my right hand, sending them along their way. "Brother Chris and I will remain here to supervise." The three of them laughed and gave a wave in return.

Several minutes later they were headed back up the incline. Ethan, who never seems to tire, was jogging toward us carrying the heavy crowbar high over his head; a big grin on his face.

"What happened?" I inquired.

"Oh, he's stuck but good," Ethan said, "no telling what he did to that Toyota underneath. We left them some water and Levi's driving to the Saucedo after we get back to camp."

I didn't say a word.

Levi was following along behind with the larger-sized Joe at his side. "I can't believe," he stated half-facetiously, "that the three of us in the military went down to help while the preacher and the retired trooper just sat there."

"Stupidity on someone else's part no longer constitutes an emergency on mine," I reasoned in return.

"You mean you'd just leave them down there?" questioned my older son.

"No, not at all. But I was going to give him enough time to ponder the errors of his ways. Next time he might not be so lucky."

Levi smirked out of the side of his mouth and shook his head, murmuring something to Joe, who looked up at me and chortled, his eyes a-twinkling. These two were an unlikely pair: the big-chested, blonde-haired Joe a perfect reflection of his strong Scandinavian heritage and Minnesota upbringing, while the darker, lean-framed Levi was a rawhide tough example of West Texas born and bred. Joe wanted to be a Navy surgeon; Levi a Marine fighter pilot. Both would argue with a tree stump and often did, the stump being represented by the other part of the duo. Yet after four years together at Annapolis, each had determined there were few closer in spirit than this polar opposite of himself.

We put away the tools, fired up the GMC, and headed for camp. While the rest of us began preparing supper, Levi and Joe drove to park headquarters at the Saucedo and informed them of the situation at the hill. They also informed the authorities about the five hikers last seen headed into The Solitario. In about an hour they were back, followed shortly by a TPWD four-wheel-drive blasting by our camp en route to the hapless black minivan.

With everyone back together and having eaten our fill, we planned for tomorrow. Levi wanted another shot at getting to the top of Fresno Peak, approaching it from the east by coming down Burnt Camp Trail. We decided to take his Suburban to the Burnt Camp Trailhead and launch out from there, allowing us the opportunity to make doubly certain those hikers from the day before had made it safely back to their vehicle.

The sun came up next morning with varying cloud cover, and a light haze had settled upon the area. When we got to Burnt Camp Trailhead there were no other vehicles to be seen; evidently the five hikers had been able to make it here and drive away. I think all of us gave an inner sigh of relief at that summation, though exposure to the elements and drinking from that infested water-hole would probably have them feeling puny for the next couple of days. I idly speculated on what wild tales they might regale others with upon their arrival back home.

We saddled up and began traipsing in a westerly direction down the trail leading to Burnt Camp. To be more precise, this way had started out as a trail in the late nineteenth century before being converted into a wagon road and was now more like a disused jeep track. The ramshackle route bends south and ultimately turns back toward the east again before ending in the main creek leading into the Lower Shutup. In effect, you are circling along the western boundaries of the The Solitario's basin, from north to south, the track winding hither and yon through the corresponding ridges of the mountain range.

At the westernmost part of this loop, Burnt Camp Trail goes through a long-abandoned site known as Burnt Camp. It and McGuirk's Tanks are the two oldest manmade landmarks in The Solitario, having been there for well over a century. In fact, early on in his career the famous western writer Louis L'Amour wrote a short story about this location, appropriately entitled *Battle At Burnt Camp*.

But for some reason lost upon me, the state park service refers to Burnt Camp these days as *Papalote Ramon*, which in the Mexican regional dialect means "Ramon's Windmill." Now I do not have a clue who Ramon was, but every map and written record I know of uses the name "Burnt Camp" for this spot, save for the literature the park puts out. This is yet another example of the arbitrary changing of a terrain feature's name for some unknown purpose; history and local customs be hanged. This is unfortunate, and again leads to the aforementioned confusion when correlating park information with everything else ever put into print about The Solitario.

At Burnt Camp you can still see where a cabin or a line shack once stood, as well as an antique Aermotor windmill, some water troughs, and a rock tank not far above the site. In construction the windmill appears to be much like the remnants of the one at the Tres Papolotes campsite, which was later replaced by an electrical pump before it too went to seed. This particular Aermotor design dates back to the late 1910s, so it is hard to determine just how long this windmill has been here. Burnt Camp is also where the lost trail that once ran mainly along the north side of the Righthand Shutup dead-ended.

From here the track parallels a draw emptying into the watershed that leads to the crevice containing Los Portales, and then on into Fresno Canyon. This narrow cut is supposed to be passable on foot, but I have never personally walked it out. It was also the canyon that Levi, Ethan, and Joe partially scouted during their first day here, and all three reported it could be even rougher than the Righthand Shutup route.

About a half mile further our group split into two parts as Levi peeled off to climb the summit of Fresno Peak. Joe and Brother Chris decided to join him on his little expedition, while Ethan and I elected to follow Burnt Camp Trail to its terminus at the main creek leading into the Lower Shutup. We would all meet back at Levi's Suburban later in the afternoon.

Continuing up the trail, Ethan and I took in the sights and made notes of what was around us. The earlier haze had lifted, giving way to a partly cloudy day with the viewing conditions that arid regions are known for. We walked among rolling hills, interspersed with sections of roughhewn terrain that appeared to have been cut from the whole by some enormous rock-eating chainsaw. From time to time, when the path went over a low pass, we could catch glimpses of the other three making their way to the top of Fresno Peak.

As we skirted the desolate foothills along the northeasterly side of Fresno Peak, the land began to fall away from us, and the track dipped towards the lower elevations to the east. A small solitary pipeline ran alongside, rusted from decades upon decades of exposure; evidently it had brought water from the Burnt Camp area to long-emptied livestock troughs along the way. The paralleling pipeline ended near where the trail entered a junction of small ravines just southwest of Needle Peak.

There we found another reason for the water pipeline. Though little remained in the vicinity, it appeared that some sort of camp had been constructed here a long time ago. My best guess was the spot provided temporary living quarters for those involved in the diggings of this general area, and most likely why the trail had carried wheeled traffic in a bygone era. Exploratory diggings along with full-fledged mine shafts are more common in The Solitario than one might first believe; the tumultuous geological activities forming these mountains gave some men the idea that precious metals were there for the taking just below ground. But to my knowledge none of their mining attempts ever worked out financially, and all that is left to speak of their efforts are these decaying sites.

From here a hiker or backpacker can turn down the creek and follow it into the Lower Shutup. Since Ethan and I had already wandered that direction on previous trips, we maintained our course where the trail comes out of the wash at the foot of Needle Peak. There we took our nooning among a stand of boulders providing partial shade against the midday sun. We were sitting among them enjoying lunch when I glanced toward Fresno Peak and saw three tiny figures silhouetted on its summit against a brilliant blue sky. Levi and company had reached their goal.

I pointed them out to Ethan, who borrowed my binoculars to take a better look. Some two years younger than Levi and of an even more muscular build, he and his older brother personified those proverbial two sides of the same coin. Good-natured and easygoing with a temper slow to show, Ethan had followed his older brother through Eagle Scouts, UIL championships, graduating valedictorian, and then on to Annapolis. Yet having done so, he still managed to put his own brand on every accomplishment they shared, and then go on to others they didn't. Now he was a very capable, multi-talented leader of other men as well as an excellent traveling companion, and I was glad for his company.

The two of us finished our meal of MREs, shouldered our gear, and leaned into the harness again as we headed along the trail. Moving out of the creek bed the weathered track tops out, affording a commanding view of the Lower Shutup watershed as well as the lower eastern side of the basin in The Solitario. It was like having the world unto ourselves, as nothing stirred in any direction for as far as the eye could see.

Descending in elevation again from the higher divide, the path winds to and fro as it passes through a sagging gap, a no-longer-needed opening in a rusting, partially collapsed fence line which looked to have been there since at least the early part of the past century. Moving through, the route continues to snake along roughly east, sloping off toward the main feeder for the Lower Shutup before turning northerly and joining that same creek bed.

Here are more signs of how men once tried to extract their earthly fortunes from the hard, unyielding ground beneath their feet. Nearby is the abandoned carcass of an old wood stove, joined by a disarray of bricks, tin cans, discarded coiled cables, and the metal rims from an old wagon. Off to the side are the tattered remains of a stock pen, rusting barbed wire now loosely draped between wood posts that do well to stand upright against the encroaching desert. There is no mark on a map I am aware of, no page in a book or diary to tell what happened here or how long ago it was. But at some time this bric-a-brac display of discarded articles was of real importance to the affairs of some men. Quietly Ethan and I passed on, observant to an open graveyard of someone else's dreams.

About a quarter of a mile up the creek bed is an intersection of well-defined trails marked by the park. The one running in a northerly fashion goes on to the Tres Papalotes campsite, while the other forks off northwest and ultimately ends at the Burnt Camp Trailhead. The state park refers to it as the Inner Loop of the Solitario, while the Burnt Camp Trail is also named the Outer Loop. We took this Inner Loop to bring us back to Levi's Suburban and where we had started from that morning.

Though these days it is easily the best known, one should not assume the Inner Loop is the only path wandering through this part of the Solitario. There are others, dating back to the dawn of the twentieth century, that crisscrossed through the immediate area. Now at an age where their disused remnants have been mostly reclaimed by nature, each one had its own purpose and story which have been lost to time and the desert.

Some three quarters of a mile up the Inner Loop you come across one of these routes heading due south off a finger of high ground. Newer than most of the others, it is fairly easy to spot when it leaves the main track. Moreover its purpose is clear: at the end of the short spur is a mineshaft of sorts. But *quien sabes* what the unknown miners were looking for, or whatever happened to them. It is the way of this land, for each new discovery there are at least a dozen more unanswered questions linked to it.

Another half mile or so the Inner Loop climbs through a low pass before descending into a narrow ravine that should be a "must see" for anyone venturing into this basin. Not very long nor very deep, it nevertheless will delight the inquisitive with the sheer amount of agate rock found along both walls as well as in its floor. We took our time making our way through, studying the various outcroppings as well as the veritable piles of the stuff that we were walking upon. To experience this rare sight was in itself worth the trip. Most probably as many others have done, we immediately christened the cut "Agate Canyon."

A short distance beyond the ravine was a large earthen dike, constructed to collect any runoff coming out of the crevice's mouth. Decades ago this was apparently a ranch camp, as there was a set of old pens on the opposite side of the trail. Like most every other spot for water collection we had visited, it was bone dry, an undeniable testament to the importance of carrying your own water while in this isolated, thirsty land.

From there it was just a short hop to Levi's truck at the trailhead, ending an easy day of about ten miles on foot. Levi, Joe,

Cliffs of Fresno Canyon and beyond to The Solitario

and Chris arrived shortly thereafter, having come pretty much straight across country from Solitario Peak, using the creek beds and natural terrain contours to chart their course. Other than the members of our little party we had seen no one else, which in itself made for a very good day. After briefly sharing some of our escapades with each other, we loaded up and headed back to camp.

That night after supper I lay in the darkness, thoughtful. There is much to be considered in the quiet of a high desert night, away from the noise of technological baubles which seem to master us rather than we them. The lessons garnered out here are important enough for most to appreciate, but it seems that too many are so busy with the constant distractions of modern life they don't have the time to mull them through.

I thought of those who we had come into contact with the day before. It is a tradition in our family to refer to such as "pilgrims," denoting individuals who blunder into a new and demanding environment, usually wholly underprepared for the difficulties involved. My wife of many years says this is why so many campgrounds are situated in the bottoms of mountainous areas, because "pilgrims fall off in the dark." I wondered if those whom we had encountered learned anything from their assorted predicaments. Some wit once remarked that experience is often something you get after you needed it.

Yet the truth is that most all of us have been pilgrims at some point in our lives, whether we care to admit it or not. The word in itself should not be anything to be ashamed of; it just means we were inquisitive enough to step out of our own little dwarflike comfort zones and try something new, perhaps even somewhat perilous.

When John Bunyan wrote *The Pilgrim's Progress* in the late seventeenth century, I do not think he decided on the title lightly. For without progress in whatever pilgrim's journey we are inclined to undertake, there is nothing of consequence to be had. There are no stories, no memories, no lessons learned, and no inner sense of growth or achievement. And most likely, no real happiness with who we are down deep inside.

That would be a mournfully sad epitaph to the precious little time we have on this earth, as well as the priceless gift of life that God so graciously grants us. May we all be pilgrims at some time in our existence, headed for the promised land.

CHAPTER 7

Surprises

Insanity is relative. It depends on who has who locked in what cage.

—RAY BRADBURY

I knew he was hanging around someplace close; I'd seen his sign and that had been more than enough to serve notice of his presence. I had been scouting along an eroding lip of the canyon wall when I first spied his leavings. Fresh urine; hadn't even had time to start evaporating on this warm, breezy day. What got to me most was that he had been so bold in the act; anyone looking up from the bottom or across the flat from the east could not have missed him silhouetted against the afternoon sky.

Like I said, I knew he was close. Standing on that lip I had to admire his choice for a view. From this point you could see Study Butte, Terlingua, Lajitas Mesa, and a lot of country in between. The beige sandstone bluffs cut by Terlingua Creek served as the centerpiece for a picture of what makes this land so special. To my right and forming that side of the frame were the multihued low hills that feed Willow Creek, which corkscrews down to lose itself into the larger Terlingua. To my left was the jumbled terrain of the ominously named Rattlesnake Mountains, and the top of this frame was formed and then finished by a crystal blue sky.

Over my shoulder rose the Chisos Mountains, some of the highest in Texas and home to a veritable oasis for plants and animal life not normally found in the unforgiving Chihuahuan Desert. At any point on the compass were other mountains, great and small of all sorts of colors, shapes, and sizes. If big cats can appreciate anything akin to natural beauty, then this sightseeing

Above the Valenzuela

gato was a regular connoisseur for the breed.

That's right, my erstwhile neighbor within a few hundred yards of my new camp was a mountain lion, and a fair-sized one at that. He was only one of very many roaming around this country, yet you do not usually find them in such close proximity while taking an afternoon stroll. However, Lady Luck does sometimes smile demurely and toss you that special hand.

Such was the case for today. I was in the Big Bend again, in a far western corner of the national park near an almost-forgotten entrance to a ranch known by very few as the Valenzuela. Like my wraith-like feline compatriot, I was just moseying around the area and taking in the local sights.

Some fifty years ago the Valenzuela was one of the places my family leased in a never-ending battle to scratch out a living down here. The ranch's name came from a prior owner, Felix Valenzuela, who was born in northern Mexico during the early 1880s. A hard worker with the intelligence and foresight to match, he owned one of the freighting companies that moved mostly mining supplies and equipment between the railroad and Terlingua, among other regional locales.

His was a successful operation, and out of the half dozen or so like companies, Valenzuela had the largest and most prosperous.

Having first started with Studebaker wagons pulled by teams of Mexican mules, he later made the transition to heavy trucks as they became more powerful and dependable. An entrepreneur with various business interests, Valenzuela used a fair amount of his hard-earned wealth to buy this place, which he christened *Rancho El Burro*.

But Felix Valenzuela was not only a prosperous and forward thinking businessman, he was also respected and trusted for his integrity by Mexican and Anglo alike. This sterling reputation led to him being elected to the office of constable for the southern part of Brewster County in 1929. Felix Valenzuela was a living, breathing example of what the United States of America is all about, the kind of man always in large demand and in such short supply.

His success story ended violently along a darkened roadway in June 1938, when he was shot to death by a bootlegger during a traffic stop near Terlingua. Ironically enough, the killer who pulled the trigger escaped justice by fleeing into northern Mexico, the same area where the constable had come from all those years before. Valenzuela was buried in Terlingua, and his tomb is still one of the larger ones to be found in the local cemetery.

By the 1960s few if anyone knew of the murdered lawman or why that ranch adjoining national park property was called "The Valenzuela." That is, until a Fort Worth area peace officer found a Brewster County Constable's badge in a flea market and decided to do some investigating. Thanks to that officer's out-sized sense of obligation to a fallen brother of long ago, the over-looked personal history of a man well worth remembering was brought to the forefront again. Today, Felix Valenzuela's name is inscribed on the National Law Enforcement Officer's Memorial in Washington, DC.

In my years of growing up in the Big Bend, the Valenzuela was the catalyst of many a fond memory for me. I took my first real deer hunting trip there, and we occasionally ran some cattle on the place. There were also burro roundups for which the ranch served as a handy launching point. These forays onto federal land were actually a National Park Service project; someone in the faraway halls of power had decided that the burro was not indigenous to the area, so they all had to go. As I recall, those were the only times when my family did not enter the park surreptitiously. My grandfather had an abiding disgust for most anything connected to the federal government, especially park rangers and the park service.

Now anybody who knows anything about burros will tell you they don't take well to being forced into anything they don't want to do. Toss in the nature of the terrain and the fact that the burros were the home team, and you can get a general idea of how much money we actually made on that little deal. As some sure-enough cowboys stretching back for generations, we prided ourselves on our mounts and our ability to ride them over this rough, rock-studded country. Yet we might as well have been trying to put a loop on Mister Gato himself for all the good we did on those forays. You know, I can't remember rounding up one single burro during that venture.

Those episodes brought on an epiphanic moment in which I decided to trust my own two feet over any four-legged creature alive. They also helped me develop an abiding admiration for those wily and self-sufficient burros. These days there is a great deal of consternation again about the presence of them in our parklands. I have heard reasoned, well-thought-out-arguments on the subject from both sides. Still, I can hardly see how it could ever really be the Big Bend without some wild burros drifting about someplace.

Anyway here I was, reliving the childhood memories of a skinny little kid who had once roamed this region and loved it more than any other place on earth. Today was only my first afternoon back, and I had already stumbled upon one of my family's old tormentors, in broad daylight no less. You see, Mister Gato and his meat-hungry kinfolk just about ate us out of house and home during our ranching activities here. My granddad, Bennie English, was of the opinion that we should send a bill to the National Park Service for keeping their pet cats so well fed on our domestic livestock. Ours was not a unique situation for the ranching communities of the Big Bend; predatory cats are still a devilish problem in these opening decades of the twenty-first century.

I circled around, keeping a watchful eye out. Trouble is that mountain lions are real good at circling, too. Their circles can often encompass a seventy-five or even hundred-mile radius when out on the prowl. But be it big loops or small, they do favor that maneuver. Stories abound about cats circling around behind their would-be pursuers, just to see what those pursuers might be up to. Call it professional curiosity if you will.

For the next hour I made my way along the floor of this small arroyo and the tributaries feeding into it. All the while I kept getting the distinct feeling of being watched. I kind of intuitively knew by what, but exactly from where was the sixty-four-thousand-dollar question. From time to time I would stop and casually scan the eastern ridge, hoping he would skyline himself again, as he had before I found his urine. Yet there was absolutely nothing to be seen or heard that would make you believe a big cat was within twenty miles of here.

I went about my business, studying the soft spots in the bottoms for tracks. There were signs of a lot of different critters passing through this small cut, but no telltale paw print of a big cat, from what I could discern. As the shadows grew longer and the sun began to sink, I decided it was time to climb out of the steep-walled wash and head back for camp.

Choosing a likely finger angling off from the high ground, I started making my way up. No sooner had I topped out than my eye caught the blur of gold and tan and beige fur moving through the brush at about a hundred yards out, covering ground at a blistering speed with no wasted motion, and with nary a sound to speak of its passing.

He was gone before it even fully registered on me what that brief flash had been. It was Mister Gato, flying low and fast for parts unknown. Mountain lions are renowned for their sprinting abilities, and this particular cat had put on a real show of it. My best guess is he had been watching me from that canyon lip all the while, and had either grown tired of the game or felt I was getting just a little too close.

Or maybe somehow that big cat knew that many years ago a certain skinny little kid had wandered these same mountains, and just wanted to give him an impromptu fly-by as a welcome back home.

The next morning found me filling up canteens and double-checking my maps after laying waste to a huge breakfast. Today was going to be a hot one, even though it was the middle of February. I was shifting campsites daily, and this evening would be moving down to Terlingua Abaja to stay the night there. While en route my plans included scouting the western and southern parts of the Rattlesnake Mountains, which I had not seen much of since leaving this country as a teenager.

Some folks might consider the Rattlesnakes little more than

South of the Rattlesnake Mountains

hills, but they are made up of some tough country and are aptly named. The smart way to get on top is by approaching from the east among a series of inclines and rises. Every other access is nearly straight up at some point, with an intriguing set of small, steep arroyos with numerous vertical runoffs and dry waterfalls. Many of these approaches consist of shale-like loose rock, which can crumble and give way underfoot, along with all sorts of unstable slides. Taken together they will test the mettle of man or beast, or rattlesnake for that matter.

After parking "Brute," my old Dodge three-quarter ton, in a secluded branch of Alamo Creek, I strapped on my gear and set a course for the Rattlesnakes. Approaching from this angle gives a person access to another good place to hike over these uplifts if you have a mind to, a dry wash that winds down from the range's southeast corner. But doing so was not on my agenda for today, and I angled away from that general area. There was a dry waterfall and cave farther west I wanted to see again, and I made them my first goal for this particular walkabout.

Walking toward the Rattlesnakes from the south takes you through as dry and bare a section of the national park as you might want to find. There are portions of this miles-wide flat where hardly anything grows; not even the hardy and widespread

Cave in dry pour off

greasewood can survive in some of these spots. When you come upon the dry waterfall, you have no idea of what you are about to see until you venture to the very edge of the flat along a low ridge about two hundred yards away. Since the cave sits near the bottom of the runoff, you don't see it until you actually drop into the odd-shaped bowl where it is situated.

Calling this indentation a "cave" is probably a stretch in the strictest sense of defining the word; it is more of an eroded cavity some four feet high and ten feet wide, with a back wall several feet deep from the face. It's a place that usually stays cool and shady on the hottest of days—a good location to rest when the sun becomes unmerciful in this taxing desert. It is also a likely spot to look for water when the infrequent rains come to this parched land.

For those seeking a less-traveled entry into the interior of the Rattlesnakes, the creek bed above the dry waterfall affords you the opportunity. The runoff's watershed leads to the very heart of the mountain range and its northern rims, and is easier walking than any other route I know of. However, the trick is in getting to the creek bed itself, either by scaling the sheer drop-off or by ascending the steep slopes on either side. Not impossible by any means, but you had better be surefooted and really wanting to

Arroyo in the Rattlesnakes

get up there.

Since I had already been in that area several times before and was by myself on this trip, I elected to stick to the lower elevations and skirt the very edges of this uplift, angling my track toward Terlingua Creek. My plan was to get to the Terlingua and walk as far as I could upstream before my allotted time ran out and I was forced to turn around. It had been a lot of years since I had last ventured that way, and there was a want inside me to revisit some of the backdrops of my youth.

Ambling along one can't help but be intrigued by the contours and colors of the terrain encountered through this stretch. It strikes the viewer as being almost a microcosm of the Big Bend itself; the *Despoblado* of ancient adage, described as where God put everything He had left over when creating the rest of world.

Trekking in this direction, one can better understand the full meaning behind that old saying. The terrain is tinted a multitude of hues, including shades of red, yellow, black, brown, tan, and gray that collide and combine with each other, resulting in an exotic landscape sprinkled with the green of greasewood, yucca, and mesquite that dot the land like the spots on a fine Appaloosa horse. There is a bewildering variety of cacti present, either out in the open or hiding among the boulders, crevices, and dry washes descending from the fragmented western pillars of the Rattlesnakes, standing quietly against the sky like slowly collapsing sentinels as eons of erosion rot them away. It may be desolate, it might even be forbidding, but if I had my choice of a place to lie down and die this would be as likely as any, my remains wasting into the ground along with those stone sentinels up above.

Before dropping into the wide expanses of the Terlingua Creek basin, you can gain enough elevation to look west across Anguila Mesa, including the mesitas atop it such as Canyon Flag and the Three Sisters. It makes for an excellent observation point to study the eastern shoulders of this massive butte from afar, and to fully appreciate its jumbled composition of foothills, canyons, cliffs, and splits. Anguila Mesa is a slice of the Big Bend all unto itself, a fearsome example of what makes this country what it is and a torturer of men many times over when the weather turns hot.

Once in the creek bed I turned north and mostly kept between its banks. At this point you are beyond the park boundaries and threading through private property, and though some of the locals pass through this area with impunity via vehicle or mountain bike, it behooves one to keep a low profile and within the natural waterway. There are homes along this portion of the creek, and between illegals and destructive trespassers, strangers are generally frowned upon.

Up the broad channel I went, past the old Franco place sitting to the west and the southern part of the Valenzuela situated on the opposite side. Above the Franco ruins was the Santa Rosa, a fairly large operation marked by the skeletons of several rock structures lying along the western bank of Terlingua Creek. The Santa Rosa was also known as the Molinar, the name of the family who once owned and worked this ranch. During the 1920s and the 1930s, the Molinar Ranch was important enough to have had a small grade school built on the site. Like the Valenzuelas, the Francos and their close kin the Molinars were involved in freighting for the mines and were well known and respected people.

It had been nearly forty years since I had last seen the Valenzuela or the Molinar up close, and the temptation was too great to resist. The remains of both have been left to the elements for many decades now; they are weather-beaten and picked over, but they are still there. The giant salt cedar that provided shade for the Valenzuela headquarters stands where it always did, but parts of it were dying away. You can still see where the buildings were,

Ruins of the old Molinar Headquarters

but what was useful and inhabitable when I was young are now only ruins. Observing them in this condition made me aware of how much time had passed, and I felt sort of weather-beaten myself.

The main Molinar headquarters was built out of native rock, and though not lived in during my lifetime, it has managed to withstand the encroaching desert better than most. I wandered around a bit, mindful of the lives that had been spent here and that I was viewing the decayed remnants of someone else's aspirations matched with back-breaking work. If you closed your eyes and listened hard, you could almost hear the children playing by the old water tank next to the long-gone adobe schoolhouse. I found myself speculating on what they would think if they could see their old playground now, and if the spirits of some ever return to the scene of their childhood for a visit.

I cleared my mind of the fog from nigh a century ago and put it back to the here and now. Easing back into the creek bed I struck out north again, leaving the thoughts and ghosts of the past behind me. I wondered if I would get another chance to see the Valenzuela and the Santa Rosa in my lifetime, and what might be left for me to recognize then.

It was right at the half-way point of my walkabout north of the

Molinar when it happened: that sinking feeling that accompanies the sudden realization the bottom of your boot is falling apart. Not all of a sudden, mind you; more like a slowly increasing flapping on the bottom of your foot as you move along. Think upon it as a rather unseemly method of incremental torture by use of a rubber sole.

Finding a suitable place to sit down, I removed the tactical boot from my left foot and examined the culprit. One look and I began singing that little ditty that goes *"You Picked A Fine Time To Leave Me, Loose Heel"* in my best Kenny Rogers impersonation. Never heard of it? Well, wait until you start losing the heel off your footwear in rough country with about seven and a half miles to go. I can guarantee that tune will pop into your head immediately.

It was already well into the afternoon and a long walk back, so I reversed course and gingerly set out for whence I had come. For the next nearly mile and a half I tried to step as carefully as possible with my left foot as I went along. But it didn't seem to matter; the heel kept pulling further and further apart, taking the rest of the tread of the sole with it. My kingdom for a roll of duct tape.

The flopping of the heel became more and more annoying. Finally, I could not stand it anymore; not only was it irksome but it was also becoming somewhat of a safety hazard. Negotiating some of this terrain was difficult enough without wondering how my left foot would hit the uneven ground next, and one misstep or miscalculation could make me a cripple a long way from where I needed to be. It was time to take some drastic measures.

Removing the offending boot, I pulled out my trusty SOG combat knife and pried the one-piece heel and tread completely off, leaving only the thin innersole. At least now I wouldn't break an ankle tripping over that flapping sole. Once done I gathered myself together and slowly started out again, trying to find a gait that would suit this newly created difference in leg length. Hobbling along with four more miles to go, I looked back as I habitually do to check my back trail. At first glance my tracks gave the impression of two different hikers: one in tactical boots and the other in slick-soled Chinese sneakers. That would definitely prey on someone's thinking until they realized what was going on.

Did I compare my field handiwork to a Chinese sneaker? Well to be honest, this little jewel had considerably less tread than that. Of course it had to be on the foot I broke about ten years ago. I distinctly recalled that orthopedic specialist shaking his head and saying the foot would never be the same, and I would probably not be able to get around on it much. Trudging my way forward, I idly wondered what he would think if he could see the miles it had covered on this one day.

I concentrated on picking out a path to steer by, careful of the infinite varieties of native plant life that can stick, poke, prod, or impale the unwary. You cannot imagine how many such plants exist in the Chihuahuan Desert until you are put into this kind of situation. Did I also mention there was no trail from Point A to Point B for my improvised route?

It was almost another mile before the inevitable occurred. I never even saw that mesquite thorn before the point plunged through the thin innersole. But I was on the ball enough to quickly shift my weight to the other side as the foot felt it push in from underneath. The barb barely made it through; thick double socks are a very good thing, and after removing the spine I was on my way again, now doubly more cautious after that close call.

With about two miles to go, I had the good fortune to come upon what was left of the main route that once ran from Castolon to what is now Terlingua. As a historical aside, a telephone line also paralleled this track, which linked the two communities together and then ran up to Alpine. Many people seem to think telephones were a fairly recent phenomenon to the lower parts of the Big Bend. Fact is, phone lines started appearing in the region before the dawn of the twentieth century. Yet with all this trivia whirling around in my brain, what mattered most now was that these dilapidated traces of roadway made for easier going.

While tiptoeing along my personal "Trail of a Thousand Pricks," something colored a lurid blue caught my eye. It appeared trapped in a small clump of stunted mesquite, and I approached it warily, expecting another thorny ambush to pick up where the last one left off. The object in question turned out to be a kid's kite, and it had come to ground a long way from wherever it was first launched. I gathered up the tattered residues and continued on, the scraps of the blue kite in one gloved hand and the sole of my tactical boot in the other. To the casual observer, I might have appeared to be a cross between Mad Max and the lead contestant in some sort of nutty scavenger hunt.

Finally, I arrived back at my truck where I stripped my gear off and placed it wearily in the floorboard of the three-quarter ton. It felt really good to crawl into that cab, sit in a cushioned seat, and take the load off my badly abused left foot. Starting the engine, I noted the thermometer indicated it was 95 degrees on this February late afternoon. Oh well, better unseasonably hot than bone-chilling cold any day. As far as my unexpected tread separation, there was really little lasting damage done other than a slight list to the port side when I stood up. The one good thing coming out of the deal was that my left foot was now definitely lighter than the right one. Or maybe that was just my imagination.

But unbeknownst to me, far grander challenges for my imagination lay on the near horizon. A few minutes later, I was pulling my old Dodge into the primitive camp sites at Terlingua Abaja when I was struck by the image of a young German tourist showering buck naked beside his genuine Volkswagen camper bus. More so, his demeanor at my approach was slightly less than completely disinterested, as if this was a normal state of affairs for him. Just when I think I've seen everything . . . then I do see EVERYTHING.

Or so I thought. Tired, hot, thirsty, and definitely sore-footed, I decided that in the best interest of international relations I should ignore this little spectacle and get my camp set up before night fell. Try to imagine my surprise some ten minutes later when I glanced over and observed two young women going through the same routine, in the same state of attire or lack thereof.

For a long moment the thought lingered in my mind that I just might be hallucinating all of this, and in reality was still lying back there among one of those rock slides with a knot on my noggin about the size of Kansas. But my left foot ached far too much for this to have been a delusion. Besides, this was one instance I was sure my God-given imagination simply wasn't up to the task of creating.

By now I was hearing the soundtrack for *Oh Brother, Where Art Thou* playing in the back of my head. Knowing there would be many potential disbelievers in regard to such a rare phenomenon, my initial inclination was to snap a photo. Then I thought better of it; anyone else remotely interested in what was transpiring here could believe whatever they wanted to. The sun was setting, I was hungry, and I did not need any more complications standing in the way of eating a well-deserved hot meal.

You can log this particular day in as being fifteen miles worth of surprises, with a real grand finale at the end.

The following day broke chilly in the pre-dawn, and I was moving slowly along the eastern bank of Terlingua Creek. I was trying to work the soreness out of that foot because I had another full day planned, albeit at a slower pace due to my present circumstance in footwear. During this warm-up lap I observed the fresh tracks of a motorcycle being ridden in places where it shouldn't have been, including right through some of the ruins located in the immediate area. The tread configuration belonged to some sort of dirt bike.

Coincidentally enough, my neighboring German "shower kommandoes" had two dirt bikes in their possession, parked alongside their Volkswagen camper bus. Without much fanfare I marched myself over to their lodgings, prepared to read them a Texas-sized riot act about disrespecting other peoples' historical landmarks; especially those situated in my favorite part of the world.

However, a quick examination of their tires found them innocent of any such wrongdoing. Curious, one of them walked up hesitantly and asked in broken English why I was looking at their dirt bikes. I briefed them on the situation and they nearly ran backwards trying to explain in both German as well as their idea of English that it wasn't them. They said they had also seen the tire tracks and were concerned they might be blamed for it. We had a pleasant conversation as far as our language difficulties would allow, and got to breaking down our respective camps.

I was near finished packing up mine when I heard the sound of a motorcycle coming down the park road which dead ends at the sites. He was at a distance and I was looking into the sun, but I could see it was a smaller motorcycle that appeared to be white or light silver in color. As soon as he saw our vehicles he came to an abrupt stop, sitting there for a moment and gunning his engine. Suddenly he reversed course, spinning his rear tire and roaring back up toward Maverick Road.

I looked at those Germans tourists and they looked at me, and we both thought the same thing. They began pointing at the disappearing motorcyclist and back to the ruins where I had found the tire tracks, gesturing and making some strong sounding accusations in their Teutonic tongue. It didn't take much imagination to guess what they were trying to say. Not bad folks, even if they did like to shower in the nude for any available audience passing through.

Shortly thereafter I had my camping equipment stowed away securely in Brute and was on the road again, though not for very far. We arrived at a likely de-embarkation point and I left the three-quarter ton parked off the side of the road. Shouldering my pack load, I pointed myself west and headed back towards Terlingua Creek.

Many assume that Terlingua Abaja was the only settlement of its kind around here, but in actuality that is far from the truth. There are decaying remains of dwellings, corrals, threshing circles, and small cemeteries scattered along this watershed reaching up as far as Hen Egg Mountain, nearly twenty miles to the north. Wandering the shoulders of Terlingua Creek, you never know when you might encounter the leftovers of someone else's efforts in attempting to extract a living from this arduous land.

Strolling along I took it easy on what remained of my left slick tire, choosing my route carefully. On occasion I would go to high ground, glassing the surrounding land for anything unusual and just getting a better feel for the area. The last portion of my second novel takes place along these banks, and I needed a memory refresher. As so often happens, there was no trail going where I wanted to go, so I made use of what was there and cut my own to do the rest.

That is until I switched from an east-west axis line to a north-south one. There I found more sign of human activity along the banks of that creek than I could ever remember. Running to and from the river were footprints in a wide-ranging variety of styles and sizes in both boot and shoe, along with the tracks of possible pack animals and some ATVs. The ATV tire marks were along the boundaries of the park and most likely belonged to the Border Patrol, as well as the shod horse tracks I found. The origin of the foot traffic was a different matter entirely.

The eight miles or so of the Rio Grande below the mouth of Santa Elena Canyon forms some of the best locations in the region for the smuggling of most anything into or out of Texas. It has been used for hundreds of years to smuggle captured slaves, stolen livestock, guns, bootleg liquor, candelilla wax, illegal drugs, and people in search of a better life, as well as most anything else that will bring an American dollar or Mexican peso. There are families on both sides of this river for whom smuggling has been a sustaining tradition reaching back for generations. They take peculiar pride in that history and the accompanying neces-

The Rio Grande at mouth of Santa Elena Canyon

sary skills needed to ply their trade successfully. Furthermore, this time honored way of life is not likely to change around here anytime in the near future. There are all sorts of laws and regulations regarding this subject on both sides of the border, but the law which reigns supreme is one of the oldest: that of supply and demand.

For example, just on the other side of the river is an isolated village by the name of Santa Elena de Ejida. The official story has always been it is a farming community making use of the fertile ground found in the adjoining flats close to the Rio Grande. And yes, there are many fields of crops located around to prove out that story. Yet the biggest part of the local economy there since the time of the great Comanche raids has always been smuggling, a fact that both national governments in the past have gone to some lengths to either deny or ignore. You can reach your own conclusions on what is what, and which economy brings by far the most monetary gain to all parties involved.

I spent the better part of the day hobbling up and down Terlingua Creek, prowling mostly along its banks. However, after about seven miles what remained of that left boot was ready to pack it in, and my left foot was in total agreement. Not only was I walking with a list, but the bottom of that foot was getting really tender from the lack of cushion and support. So I set course back to where I left Brute parked along Maverick Road, and we drifted north for our new campsite at Croton Spring.

Along the way I stopped to check on a couple of graves lying just off the roadway, situated near some adobe ruins. No one really knows who lies in either, though some say they belong to two of Gilberto Luna's wives. Luna seemed to have had the knack of outliving most everyone else in the country, and in 1947 finally passed away in Alpine at the reported age of 108. His home, a local landmark and tourist attraction known as Luna's Jacal, is located at the foot of Peña Mountain about a mile south of the graves. This primitive dwelling provided shelter for his numerous wives, as well as his even more numerous offspring, who reportedly numbered in the dozens. There has been much said and written about Gilberto Luna, yet considering the scantiness of his life's records little of it seems to have any verifiable basis. Much like the land in which he lived, the facts concerning his life have been obfuscated by rumor and speculation.

There was still some daylight left when I pulled into the Croton Spring campground. This site is right off the highway leading from Panther Junction to the west park entrance, and is one of the easiest primitive campsites to get to. Since my foot had been taking a breather during the drive over and felt a little better, I spent the next hour or so easing up the nearby creek, which runs from Croton Peak itself. The spring had water, as it usually does this time of year; a pretty spot, and the time of the evening made it more so. Small ponds seeped among the rocks and gravel beds bleached white by calcium deposits, while tufts of knee-high grass crept in from the banks to feed upon the life-giving moisture. It was a quiet place to pause and reflect on, peaceful in a way that cannot be duplicated in any other way. The sun drooped lower in the western sky, and I just kicked back for a while and relaxed.

The next morning I was making a lazy stab at packing up my gear while visiting with some fellow campers who had stopped by. We were chatting about some landmarks in the park and what they might be interested in seeing when we heard a motorcycle coming. I recognized it as sounding a whole lot like the one from the morning before at Terlingua Abaja.

This time I wasn't having to look into the sun and clearly observed a silver-colored off-road bike, a larger-sized one for the breed. The motorcycle had box-style saddlebags, and the rider was dressed in a matching silver outfit with a full-faced helmet in like color. He came barreling in toward our campsites at a high rate of speed until he spied the vehicles parked about. The rider reacted by quickly coming off the throttle and rolling to a halt.

It was almost a repeat of the morning before, except he didn't come to a stop until at the barricades where the traveled part of the road dead ends. Beyond that it becomes a hiking trail leading off toward the creek bed and spring. Looking about, the rider revved the bike's engine several times; it was obvious he really wanted to thread his way through those spaced posts and continue on. But it was just as obvious that we were watching and waiting for him to do so.

The seconds ticked by before he abruptly whipped around and left the campsites even more quickly than he had come in, spinning his rear tire again as he had done at Terlingua Abaja. This time he managed to throw a fair amount of gravel on my fellow campers' late-model pickup truck and outdoor gear.

"Friend of yours?" I enquired mildly.

"No," was the terse reply, "but I sure wish I knew who that jackass was. I don't appreciate rocks being bounced off my truck."

Admittedly I was not too up on identifying the different makes and models of off-road motorcycles. However, the fellow with me was knowledgeable about them and informed me that it was a BMW. Showing my ignorance at not knowing BMW even made a dirt bike, he explained they were comparatively rare on account of being so expensive for the type. Yet once again, this incident proved my long-term theory about dollar bills and good breeding often being mutually exclusive to each other.

To confirm my strong hunch, I walked over and found the very same knobby tire track pattern as I had seen among the ruins of Terlingua Abaja. I found myself wishing to have been standing alongside that road with a good nylon rope and something sturdy to dally onto when the aforementioned jackass took off. Then again, it is probably just as well I wasn't; I might have miscalculated my throw and stretched his neck like some kind of silver-painted rubber chicken.

The distance had been too far away to get a plate number, but I still stopped by the visitor center at Panther Junction and gave a report and description. The park personnel were appreciative and said this kind of wanton destructive behavior was a rapidly growing problem. Evidently more and more loons are beginning to discover that Big Bend National Park is a large chunk of territory with few rangers to patrol it. It's the sort of situation where you find some low-class people who have no respect for much of anything, and seem to thrive upon destroying the precious things the rest of us hold dear. So the next time you are in one of our public parks and you see something, please say something.

Heading out toward Persimmon Gap, I pondered on what I had seen over the past few days. My planned solitary sabbatical had experienced far more people than I was used to on these trips, and I had the distinct impression not all of them fit the more common definition of "tourist." The primitive campgrounds in the Terlingua Creek area were booked solid, yet one could pick and choose from any of those on the eastern side of the park. I found that fact intriguing.

Another point of interest was that although the campgrounds themselves were full to capacity, you could walk a hundred yards in any direction and be greeted by a vast and blissful solitude. Some of the folks staying in those primitive sites seemed to be doing not much more than hanging around their vehicles. It makes a gent wonder if one or more of those tourists might be waiting for someone or something else to show up. Imagine that.

As I neared the boundary for the park, my chain of thought was interrupted. There were a couple of surprises to go. The first was a little elderly lady at the park exit who started waving her arms and bouncing up and down like a high school cheerleader, trying to flag me over. I brought Brute to a screeching halt, and she excitedly exclaimed that her husband was with their disabled RV about three miles north, and she needed to get a message to him. You could tell from her accent that she was not from these parts and was feeling a bit lost in more than one way. Of course I obliged.

Some three miles later the disabled RV proved easy enough to locate. One reason was that it had broken down on a stretch of highway as straight as an arrow. Another reason was that it still sat right in the middle of the northbound lane. As I slowed down I had another one of those possible hallucinations, or the thought that I just might be in a remake of *Oh Brother Where Art Thou* and didn't even know it.

Directly behind the RV was a lawn chair. Sitting in that chair and reclined in regal fashion was the woman's husband, stylish sunshades perched on his upturned face, taking in all of the sun the Big Bend country could provide. He was making the most of it, too, because other than those sunglasses all he had on was a teeny-weeny black speedo stretched tightly around his far too ample waist.

I reflexively began fidgeting with my digital camera, preparing for the shot of a lifetime. The Kodak came up and my index finger hovered over the button, my mind contemplating a shoot/ don't shoot situation of an entirely different order from any of my years in the Marine Corps or the Texas Highway Patrol. Then the true gravity of my near action dawned upon me, and gradually my finger moved away and I put the camera back down.

There are some things you will always remember, maybe even talk about on occasion. But it just makes good sense not to leave any physical evidence linking you to the crime.

CHAPTER 8

Over on the Lonesome Side

*You should not see the desert simply
as some faraway place of little rain.
There are many forms of thirst.*

— WILLIAM LANGEWIESCHE

It was the earliest part of October when I saddled up my trusty Dodge three-quarter ton and pointed the front bumper southwest towards Big Bend National Park. Several months had passed since I had been able to do so, and the siren song of those mountains and desert had been echoing in my head during most of that time.

I was well prepared for what lay in front of me: I had my food, maps, emergency and survival supplies, plenty of fresh water, and a full thirty-seven-gallon tank of gas after a quick stop at the Chevron in Fort Stockton. I also had a plan to visit one of the more remote and desolate sections of the park, especially during the warmer months. It is a slice of the Big Bend pie bordered by the upper Ore Road and Telephone Canyon trail. There were also a few sightseeing detours in my mind that were in the general neighborhood.

When I arrived at the park it was mostly empty; I counted a grand total of two tourists inside the Panther Junction Visitor Center. That was a good sign as far as I was concerned; the fewer the people, the better I like it. Not that I have anything in particular against my fellow man, as long as there are not too many of them crowding me too closely when I feel the need for the high lonesome.

There was also a middle-aged park-ranger lady behind the desk, and she smiled as I walked up, perhaps glad to see the sight of some sort of customer other than your standard-issue *tourista*. We visited a bit about the weather and the lack of park visitors, and I told her I wanted the Telephone Canyon #2 campsite, which happens to sit at the western terminus of the trail itself.

"Oh," she says pleasantly, "you must really know your way around here."

"How so?" I ask.

"Because hardly anyone knows where that is, much less wants to go there during the warmer weather."

"All the more reason," says I. "Sign me up."

She took down my information and soon enough I was turning off the highway on to Dagger Flat Road. There was a UPS truck coming my direction as I did so, and I remember thinking those guys in brown actually do deliver most anyplace.

That would be the last vehicle or human being I would see for nearly four days.

Telephone Canyon Campsite #2 straddles a long-discarded roadway once used to haul unrefined ore from the tramway terminal, north of present-day Rio Grande Village, up to the railway at Marathon. To get there you take Dagger Flat Road and turn south where it is intersected by the Old Ore Road, which takes you past some ruins near McKinney Springs. This route is rough and high clearance vehicles are a must, preferably with four-wheel drive or a good two-wheel mechanical locker. You can also access this campsite by taking the highway toward Rio Grande Village and turning north at the lower entrance for the Old Ore Road. That way is not nearly as hard on a vehicle and makes for an easier drive, but it is considerably longer.

The campsite itself sits at the northwestern foot of Alto Relex. No one is quite sure where the name for this peculiar mesa came from or what it is supposed to mean. Furthermore, no one is even really certain what language was used to coin its name. The *alto* part is simple enough as it can mean *tall* or *high* in Spanish, but the *relex* seems to have everyone stumped. I have heard some say it is Greek, others speculate it sounds like Latin. But nobody seems to be able to translate it. In the end, the name and its meaning are most probably yet another one of those mysteries of the Big Bend never to be fully solved or explained.

What is known about this secluded mesa is that it towers a good thousand feet over the Old Ore Road, ringed by bluffs up to hundreds of feet high on both sides. Some four miles long and

The Alto Relex

nearly a mile at its widest point, the only accessible routes to the top are along its northern and southern tips. Both routes can be a real scramble.

After setting up camp, I decided to hike north along remnants of the aforementioned road, which was specifically constructed for transporting large amounts of raw ore coming out of the Boquillas, Mexico, mines. The track presently referred to as the "Old Ore Road" north of Alto Relex was the route used for general transportation as well as the hauling of minerals before the time of the International Mining Company tramway.

The completion of this six-and-a-half-mile overhead cable system changed how and where the ore came across the river, and another roadway was built to facilitate its movement from the tramway terminal just southeast of Ernst Basin. Once this newer, far better route was completed, hardly any ore was moved along the older track. About the only area where the two roads ran as one was along the western side of Alto Relex, at least until they joined up again some two and a half miles northeast of McKinney Springs.

Having more than one road to get to a certain destination was not an unusual situation back then. Potential obstacles, repair work, variations in weather, and the need for valuable cargo to arrive at a set place and time constituted the reasons for these alternate routes. West of Nine Point Mesa the old Terlingua to Alpine road had two different tracks, as did the lower part of the Ore Terminal route detailed in my story "Land of Broken Dreams." It was common practice during the early mining days, and pieces of these substitute ways can still be found if you know where to look.

I was particularly interested in this one, as it had been abandoned for several decades. Moreover, I had heard about an old mine around here and had noted a reference to it on some maps. Remembering the description, I figured I was close to its location and might even find a spur off this road leading me to those diggings. It is easy enough to find this track from the primitive campsite, as it runs right through the middle and heads out north. Grabbing my pack and my camera, I did the same.

The roadway angles up a small valley for the first part, paralleling an unnamed dry wash as it travels north. Walking along its decayed surface, I found numerous clues that helped tell the route's story. The first thing that struck me was the quality of work; it was far better done than the corresponding section of the Old Ore Road which runs past the McKinney ruins. It put me in mind of the lower portion of this same track as it starts into Ernst Basin, specifically the farther west branch that winds through a small canyon there. The road's foundation had been leveled and painstakingly stabilized with layers of flat rocks in several places, to keep it from giving way when up against a bluff or running alongside the creek. It was obvious why it had been the preferred route when transporting those heavy loads of raw ore.

Scattered along the way were horseshoes, rusting links of chain, nails, old tin cans, an antique Owens hub meter, and from all appearances, a burial plot of some sort. I circled around two or three times examining the site; there was little else but a large pile of rocks over six feet long and about half as wide which had been there a long time. There were no markers to be found, but it wouldn't be the first time I have come across an unmarked grave in the Big Bend.

Looking around, I could see the remains of past human habitation nearby. Lines of other rocks, old cans, pieces of wire, and other such debris littered the area. Altogether the scene was yet another fading, timeworn collection of some nameless person's failed hopes and dreams ever so slowly decomposing back whence they came. I pushed on as the daylight hours were rapidly dwindling away. Yet I was not unduly concerned about that; the terrain was easy enough to navigate, and a full moon was scheduled to rise before dark.

For a while the road rose at a fairly steady rate until it topped out in a small pass and dropped into lower ground beyond. I checked my watch and saw I had been away from camp for two and a half hours; I had only meant to be gone less than half that time. Near my turnaround point at the pass, I spied a deteriorating track that I believed to be the spur to the mine I had been looking for. It led off in the right general direction and I was sorely tempted, but I decided I had better head back to camp instead.

To help make up for the negative numbers posted on my wristwatch, I began recon shuffling along the better remaining parts of the road as daylight went away. Nearing the spot where the route entered the arroyo north of my camp, I cut off across country to save a little more time and avoid any hostile critters who might be lurking in the underbrush during the cool of the evening.

As if to prove out this little theory, I was crossing a brushy finger of that draw when I stumbled across piles of mountain lion scat on the shelf above the far bank. The droppings were old and dried up but there was plenty of it; evidently Señor Gato was fond of using this ledge as a favored spot to take unsuspecting prey.

There was also something else off to my right that caught the eye. Situated at the edge of the underbrush, it was positioned in an all-too-familiar coil neatly camouflaged by its gray and black diamondback pattern. Even in the waning cusp of twilight, it was obvious the motionless object was a good-sized rattlesnake.

But if snakes can sleep I had surely caught this one napping. His trademark triangular head was down in the middle of his coil, so still and unaware that I thought he might even be dead. Nevertheless, one rock tossed in his general direction quickly proved otherwise. It was a rattler all right, and he was very much alive. The pit viper hightailed it for the tall grass, singing his favorite "rattling bug" song as he slithered away in high gear. Finding this little patch of real estate having far too high a ratio of things that could hurt a fellow, I lit out in the opposite direction for terrain where one could better see where one was going.

Although the afterglow of the sun still burned below the western horizon, that full moon was already peeking above the craggy peaks of the Sierra del Carmen. This was a welcomed happenstance, and within another quarter of a mile I was steering by moonlight bright enough to cast a distinct shadow. Walking in this manner brought back memories from the time my family had moved from the Big Bend to Fort Stockton. The school bus would drop me off at the highway and I would hurry home, do whatever chores needed doing, and then grab my .22 rifle and stay out until well after dark. I know now it was my way of seeking solitude to figure out who I really was and why. Some feelings and needs never change, no matter how much older and more mature you become.

Once back at camp I ate supper by beam of flashlight and chewed on those thoughts, and what tomorrow might bring. The grub was simple and it was cold, but out here in this isolated stretch of desert backcountry it tasted like cuisine fit for royalty.

The next morning after breakfast I was on the move and heading up Telephone Canyon Trail. According to local lore, Telephone Canyon got its name from an Army-emplaced phone line that ran from somewhere around the Adams Ranch. Up until then it was known as Heath Canyon, and the creek running in the bottom of this large crevice still bears that name. I have found few historical notes on where the line ended on the other end, but after this little venture I would bet that it couldn't have been along the same route I used.

This trail starts out at Telephone Canyon Campsite #2 and winds its way easterly to the park boundary lying nearly seventeen miles away. There is little here to attract the average hiker in the way of either manmade or natural landmarks, nothing other than a lot of rough country which seems to form its own little secluded world. Compared to most of the other Big Bend park trails not many venture this direction, thus making it a seldom-mentioned path that few speak of or know much about.

What I can tell you about Telephone Canyon Trail is that it is rugged, it is dry, it is remote, and it was very hot during the days I traipsed along it. The oppressive heat is why most of those who try this path do so in the dead of winter, preferring the occasional frosty chill to the blisteringly high temperatures of other parts of the year. Yet early fall is when the Big Bend has its best Sunday dress on, making for a jaunt about as picturesque as any other I have taken in this part of the world. But you had better be ready to sweat for the view.

Cairn Along Telephone Canyon Trail

This episode turned out to be one of the more punishing hikes I have taken in some time. It is not for the inexperienced, the physically inactive, or the fainthearted. Rock cairns mark the way, and one needs to keep a sharp eye out for them because of the hit-or-miss condition of the trail. Some of these cairns are next to useless due to their placement, while others are prominently displayed, appearing almost as works of art when properly framed by the stark background.

You will spend time locating some of these cairns, so figure that into your schedule and don't get in a hurry; this is especially true when ascending. Given the terrain and the wild game paths that occasionally crisscross your way, it would be very easy to stray off track if you are not paying attention. It wouldn't be as easy to get completely lost, but this has been known to happen. I strongly encourage anyone taking this trip to get the necessary topographical maps and know how to read them.

I also strongly suggest that whoever is handling those maps have a good sense of direction and/or be handy with a compass. Finally, and just as importantly, make certain you have plenty of water. On this particular hundred-degree-plus day I drank over five quarts while on the trail and topped it off with nearly two more quarts of Gatorade when I got back to base camp. To be short of any of these necessities could be an open invitation to disaster.

From the campsite Telephone Canyon Trail starts out innocently enough, but within a couple of hundred yards you are traversing sheets of solid stone or scrambling through small fields of broken shale. The disheveled path calls for surefootedness; it bends and twists its way along an arroyo that you parallel up to a low pass. Near the top of this terrain feature is your first surprise: an old dam constructed of rock and mortar.

It sits in the military crest of the saddle, hidden from view until you are almost there. The dam is duly noted on the quad map for this area, yet is easily missed among the contour lines unless the map is studied carefully. As best I could estimate the structure was about twenty feet high, eighty feet long, and about five feet thick at the base. I looked around for any marker or plaque giving information concerning it, but there was none to be found. The decaying masonry hinted at a date of construction that easily could have been a century ago.

Then the thought dawned on me: just how did the unknown builders get the needed supplies and equipment up here to do this? It had to have been packed in by either mule or burro, as I could not see how you could bring in a wagon. The only other feasible route I knew of to this spot would be along the eastern side of Alto Relex through an unnamed canyon located there, and that would make for a fair distance to any road either now or back then. In the end, I was forced to chalk it up to yet another example of what those who came before us were able to accomplish without our "indispensable" modern technology. The presence of the dam also helped explain why there was a trail through here to begin with.

Beyond the dam the path smoothed out and was easier to follow, easing along as it meandered through a series of low rises and creek bottoms. To your right the cliff faces of Alto Relex become bigger and more formidable again, angling off to the south. The trail has little elevation change, and the gentle interlude lulls you into believing the challenging part may be over.

But it isn't; not by a long shot. This is canyon country, and most of the canyons run perpendicular to the trail itself. That means a certain amount of up-and-down going, and I don't mean just a little up or a little down; if the reader will take a look at the appropriate topographical map, you'll see what I mean. Plus,

Climbing up the Telephone Trail

the ever-present heat made each one of those contour lines a little more difficult to subdue as the day wore on.

The real party begins at a saddle you pass through where the path drops off abruptly into the floor of a large canyon. At the bottom you will find an intersection of routes; Ernst Basin Trail comes in from the south and dead-ends at a junction there. Telephone Canyon Trail continues on, weaving its way above the surrounding crevasses until it tops out where blue sky touches the farthest line of those barren, sun-bleached mountains sitting to the north. Be ready for some truly spectacular views, as well as some maneuvering amid broken shale and slick rock to see them.

The most treacherous ascent you make lies past where Ernst Basin Trail tees in and you begin climbing out of the canyon. It is a steep, hardscrabble grade to the top abounding in unstable rocks, slabs of slippery stone, and scrub undergrowth that will reach out to trip you at the most inopportune moment. This lively combination makes for occasional erratic footing at such an acute angle, especially with some weight on your back. It nearly proved to be my Waterloo.

During this particular hike I was alone and being more than my usual careful self. Yet in this case it didn't seem to help much, as about two thirds of the way up one of those unstable rocks gave way under my right foot in mid-stride. It was one of those sorts of situations where everything goes into slow motion, and you have plenty of time to realize what's about to happen. I toppled over backwards and hit hard on a large tier of rock situated below and behind me. The impact jarred every bone in my body, and my eyes must have spun like a Las Vegas one-armed bandit after some slot jockey pulls the lever.

I lay there sprawled out awkwardly on my back for a long minute, trying to catch my breath and taking inventory of anything that might be damaged, torn, broken, or missing. But other than being shook up and aching in several new places, all the parts issued at birth still seemed to be in proper working order. That was a very good thing, because at this point it would have been a long crawl back to camp.

My backpack, containing my emergency supplies and extra water, helped in cushioning the blow. I was also wearing a long-sleeved shirt, full-length trousers, military-issue jungle boots, a flat-brimmed felt hat, and a pair of leather gloves. A word of caution to be heeded: If you are going to challenge this country on its home court, make certain you dress appropriately for the occasion. That philosophy certainly worked for me in this circumstance.

After going through that mental checklist of issued parts, I slowly got back to my feet, now aggravated with myself more than anything else. The heat and the harsh terrain were starting to wear on me, and after that close call I slowed down even further and paid more attention to what I was doing. Nevertheless, I would slip twice more during this trip on account of the fickle fragments of rock that litter this particular path. Nearly two weeks later, I was still sporting deep bruises from my unexpected tumble.

Telephone Canyon Trail is one of those where you take the high ground in levels; what you think is the summit turns out to be just another prelude to another higher level behind it. It was physically draining, especially following my spill, and with mostly no breeze the day felt even hotter. By this juncture I knew that I wasn't going to make it all the way to Telephone Canyon, but I wanted to at least see it from a distance. You can attribute that peculiar notion to a Moses and the Promised Land complex, if you will.

View from near summit of Telephone Trail

Yet the views of the strikingly rugged landscape possess a unique beauty, making the effort to get there all the more worthwhile. The canyons are interlinked and connected to each other in a bewildering maze of colors, shadows, and angles that appear both ominous and yet beguiling. Over your shoulder the full breadth of the Chisos Mountains come into view as you climb, along with everything else from the Chilicotal over to Burro Mesa and beyond, on both sides.

After nearly five hours of steady hiking, I cleared the last shelf and started down into Telephone Canyon. I could now see the bluffs forming its northern side and walked on until I located a suitable spot to drop my pack, change socks, and eat a late lunch under a tall yucca. The shade available was pretty paltry by most standards, but there's not much else along these parts to give a man respite from the sun. On my map the contour lines for the trail ahead were not nearly as condensed as those behind, and the bottom of the chasm itself is broad, with little elevation change until it enters the Rio Grande near Stillwell Crossing. My efforts had gained me a psychological victory, if nothing else, since I had made it through the tough part. After letting my feet rest and taking in the scenery, I turned around and headed for camp.

On the way back, I came across a strange sight that had me

sitting and studying for some time before eventually realizing what it was. I had strayed from the track a bit and had wandered toward a likely overlook above the many jagged, intertwined arroyos that can be encountered on this side of Alto Relex. In doing so I noticed something odd in the next canyon over; it appeared to be light reflecting from a cave near the top of the bluff facing me. A second look revealed there were actually two somethings gleaming from inside.

The distance was nearly a quarter of a mile, so details were somewhat lacking to the naked eye. But I could plainly see the two reflections glowing in the semi-darkness, evidently caused by the rays of the mid-afternoon sun angling into the cave's mouth. Puzzled and somewhat excited, I fished out my binoculars and zoomed in on the mystery.

Of course my first instinct was to think I had made some spectacular find, like the long-elusive Lost Nigger Gold Mine, rumored to be in this general vicinity. I apologize for the use of the *n* word here to anyone who might be offended, but no one saw fit to consult me before naming it, and the label is historically correct. This fabled mine is yet another of those enduring riddles of the Big Bend, one that should not be relegated to total obscurity strictly because of a poor choice of words in describing it.

Legend tells of a black wrangler by the name of Bill Kelley who cowboyed this remote land in the later decades of the nineteenth century. Fairly well known for his abilities in the saddle, Bill made the ill-starred decision to go to work for a couple of nefarious brothers who owned a ranch in this general area. One day while in their employment, he walked up to one of them and held a large nugget under the man's nose, announcing that he had found a gold mine in the backcountry.

At first the four brothers ridiculed him; saying it was only fool's gold fit for the fool who would think it was the real article. But it was they who ended up looking like fools after confirmation was made by an assayer that the nugget was indeed a high grade of gold ore. That was when greed and avarice took them over completely, and they demanded that Bill show them where he had found his nugget. The story gets somewhat murkier, and the truth perhaps a lot uglier in the telling from this juncture forward.

Some say that Bill Kelley got scared and left West Texas entirely, never to return. Others claim the brothers tortured and then murdered him in their vain attempt to find out where the mine was located. Whatever happened, the black cowboy evidently never told them where he had found his gold-encrusted rock, and the brothers never discovered where it had come from.

That is not to say they did not try, along with a lot of other people who spent small fortunes and much of their own lives combing this desolate land in search of Bill's elusive, as well as unproven, mother lode. The search went on for at least fifty years on both sides of the river, with nary a granule of the precious dust produced by the combined efforts of all those involved.

There are those who surmise there never was a gold mine, that Bill had the rock made up to play a joke on his unscrupulous employers. If so, the gag was very costly in more ways than one, as it may have cost him his life. Whatever happened to Bill Kelley, no investigation into his disappearance was ever conducted, and no charges were ever brought against the brothers.

The moral of this little tale could be that gold fever does bring out the worst in most everyone, so if you ever find any, be very cautious about who you share your secret with. That and using the word *fool* for any reason is like casting a large golden nugget into a dirty, still pool encircled by all sorts of folks. The resulting splash can cause quite a commotion, and in ways you cannot even begin to account for. It might also get somebody killed.

Once logic had beat back a childhood spent reading about Alan Quatermain and J. Frank Dobie's *Coronado's Children*, I determined that I was not looking at a cave but rather more of a hollow in the slender canyon top. Time and erosion had formed holes leading out the opposite side of it, and I was not seeing one cliff face but rather two spaced very closely together. Those radiating somethings were actually sunlight being reflected from the face of the second canyon through those holes in the hollow of the first. It was one of those instances where one marvels at the intricacies woven into God's creation, and how much in nature is not what it appears to be at first glance.

It was late in the evening when I finally made it back to my base camp on the north end of Alto Relex. I don't know if I'll ever get the chance to travel all of Telephone Canyon Trail. Furthermore, I don't know if I would even try it again, at least in such heat while out by my lonesome. But I do know that as I sat that night scribbling lines by candlelight, dog tired, footsore, and with innumerable aches and pains lapping at my banged-up body, I was surely glad I got the chance to go at least once. It was a day not to be forgotten.

The second morning I was on the move again, though admittedly a little slower whilst working out the assorted kinks and tender spots accumulated the day before. Today I was going to take it a bit easier while doing some more reconnoitering, which had been part and parcel of my plan for this trip.

My route would basically consist of a loop utilizing part of the track I had covered previously. The idea was to follow Telephone Canyon Trail for a distance before leaving it to skirt the northeast side of Alto Relex, aiming for an unnamed canyon that Ernst Basin Trail passes through. I had been to that canyon before but from the south side, coming up to it from Ernst Tinaja. My objective was to reach the spot where I had turned around during that prior trip, thus completing the circuit. Afterwards I would take Ernst Basin Trail north to where it teed into Telephone Canyon Trail, and from there head back to camp using my path from the evening before.

The first leg along the Telephone Canyon trail was under the thinnest of hazes that gave a bit of relief from the sun, a welcome respite from the heat that was sure to come. This semishade lasted for about two and a half miles, almost to the point where I entered a draw angling toward my first objective. There its last vestiges were burned away by the morning sun, which began to shine down in earnest. The sweat from my body began to bead and pool. The draw was fairly large and easy to navigate, and in turn combined with others as they funneled into the canyon that cradles Ernst Basin Trail.

I have written before of this particular unnamed canyon, of how it twists and turns along a north-south axis running parallel to the eastern reaches of Alto Relex. You can access it from either the Ernst Tinaja area or from the Willow Tank campsites on the south end, or go in from the north as I was doing today. Either can be done in a day's hike, but you'd better step it out when you make your try.

Hardly any of this area east of Alto Relex, be it peak or creek or valley or canyon, has a name on any map. Nothing here but empty desert and gnarled landmarks shrouded in anonymity, known only to a few vicariously and by fewer still who have seen them with their own eyes. That extra time I mentioned I needed for this hike will be spent taking in these sights, as well as basking in the rare sort of solitude found in such an out-of-the-way, lonely place.

One other thing of note about this canyon: it channels the watershed from most of the country I had scouted the day before. There is literally a maze of small canyons, draws, gorges, and dry washes in this general vicinity, and if it ever decides to rain hard, the canyon can flow a torrent of water that will sweep aside or obliterate most anything in its path. This same watershed continues through Ernst Tinaja and on to where it finally dumps into Tornillo Creek just south of the ruins of La Noria. If you are prowling through any of these spots and notice heavy rain clouds to your north, your best course of action is to get out as quickly as possible.

I made the trip to the upper entrance of the canyon in good form and with nothing unusual to report, other than some eye-catching scenery found along the way. The view of the upper entrance for the canyon itself is enough to excite the imagination; there is a bluff of solid rock over fifty feet high that actually hangs over the floor of the narrow gap, as if guarding it from any passing interlopers. For those readers who might be old western movie buffs, think of *McKenna's Gold* or *Valley of the Gwangi*.

Walking past this foreboding entrance, you discover how your near world view can change dramatically. What felt relatively open and spacious becomes tightly packed and walled in after just a few steps. The broken ridges of the canyon's two faces rise up on either side, worn and eroded by the very same forces of nature that created them. Once in the gorge it didn't take me long to find where I had turned around during my previous trek. I had nearly gotten all the way through coming from the south; less than a quarter of a mile more and I would have been in open country.

Besides the striking landscape one of the other niceties about this canyon is that it matters not the time of day or the season; shade can be found within. The twisting and turning of the channel combined with the high surrounding walls afford protection from the sun at any time, regardless of where it may be positioned above. I nooned at the spot where the overhanging rock guards the north entrance; the natural awning provided a cool shade that sure felt good on this hot, dry day.

After having some lunch and airing out my feet, I started up the Ernst Basin Trail. This path runs nearly due north until it deadends into the trail for Telephone Canyon, at the same intersection mentioned yesterday. You won't find this path on many maps, and if you do, it will not usually be listed by its given name. But I have always heard it referred to as the Ernst Basin Trail, so that will be the name I shall use here. I checked my topo map and confirmed where it veered off from the main creek channel and entered yet another dry wash. There are cairns placed along the route for those who do not believe in maps, but many times the cairns are spotty in number or not clearly visible.

Not much further up, the dry wash turns into a small-sized canyon lined with heavily fractured faces of rock along both sides. The crevice is not very tall or wide but full of items of interest that will make you stop, take a second look, and consider. Craggy, split, and weather beaten, the walls of this cut gave all the indications of a good deal of instability. There were numerous signs of recent slides and rock displacements, and it was obvious there were other spots ready to go at the slightest provocation.

Making this crazy quilt of jumbled stone their home was the largest number of black rock squirrels I had ever encountered in one place in the Big Bend. Even in the unrelenting heat of the early afternoon, they flitted to and fro along the steep walls and through the fissures, reappearing for the briefest of moments before vanishing into the rocks again. If one has a particular interest in these small animals and their communal behavior, you could spend hours sitting in that arroyo observing their antics.

Just beyond the squirrels I came upon another unusual sight: the opposing faces of this portion of the canyon were dotted with an assortment of small caves and holes of every description. The largest appeared to be no more than two feet in diameter; the smallest measuring in the scantiest of inches. With no rhyme or reason they ran haphazardly along both sides of the gorge. Some were horizontal while others burrowed in at varying angles; I even saw a larger vertical one which put me in mind of a vent shaft for a mine.

As you move along, the canyon walls ebb and flow until you pass through a narrow chokepoint. Above this passageway, the gorge opens up to collect yet other canyons and runoffs that drain into it. From here I could see some of the high ground to the north I had traveled the day before. In the dry wash beds funneling into the chokepoint, stands of yucca grew in abundance,

Holes in canyon wall

along with a wide variety of other cacti and native plants.

These tall yuccas are prevalent in this region of the park, and especially in this particular watershed. While walking through this area your imagination starts playing with the shapes of these agave denizens, until some almost appear to take on individual characteristics and personalities. If you recall in the classic comic strip *Peanuts*, Snoopy had a desert-dwelling brother by the name of Spike. In his paper-and-ink isolation, Spike used to hold one-sided conversations with Arizona saguaros quite frequently. That has never happened to me with any Big Bend yuccas as of yet, save for an occasional word tossed their way during a weak moment. But if I ever hear one answer back, I would consider it an irrefutable signal to get really concerned about myself.

After another half a mile past the upper end of the arroyo, I was at the tee where Ernst Basin Trail deadends into the track for Telephone Canyon. The joining is well-marked by rock cairns, but there are no metal signs such as those seen along the more well-traveled paths in Big Bend National Park. I turned my nose toward the western sun and began the climb out; from this spot it was about three and a half miles back to my campsite.

You hardly hear anything about Ernst Basin Trail; not many know of it and far fewer have walked its path. Yet if you want to

Telephone Canyon Trail north of Alto Relex

break away from where the rest of the crowd goes and step into a quietude all your own, you could do far worse. By linking up with some of the other trails through this section of the park, one can go from the highway near Boquillas Canyon, past the old ore terminal, and all the way beyond McKinney Spring. However, anyone planning on doing so needs to go fully prepared for the trip: this is lonesome country with abrupt extremes, and help is not just the next block over.

As the sun sank below the northern rim of Alto Relex, I began the final gentle descent east of the old dam before the trail rapidly dropped off toward base camp. It was the sort of evening that is often my favorite part of the day in the Big Bend, along with the early morning sunrises. After such a scorcher the shadows start to creep out, and you first feel the faintest hints of cooler air as you walk along. It hides in pockets when the wind is still, or wafts with the breeze whichever direction it happens to blow. The sensation is pleasant in the lateness of the day and as those shadows grow longer. But cooler can be a relative term, because when the thermometer was checked back at camp, it was 97 degrees a half hour past sundown.

Tomorrow would be another day; I would be breaking camp and headed back to what is called civilization. But tonight I would lie under a full moon, bright as a reading lamp, in a place as remote and isolated as I could find, and think upon that dam at the top of the pass. It had to be nearly a hundred years old. Whoever built it was now long dead, and its purpose and exact age most likely died with them. It seems these days no matter where you go someone else has already been there before, leaving their mark in some manner for those who come along later to ponder over.

That dam was someone else's mark. I admired their perseverance and tenacity, and wondered what kind of marks they might have found when they first came to this land. A fading pictograph on a canyon wall, a broken arrowhead, or perhaps metate holes belonging to a long-forgotten campsite or people?

And in turn what did those unknown people find upon first coming here? How many times did they also wonder about some small discovery while lying under a full moon, before sleep overtook them?

In the end, only God and the desert know.

CHAPTER 9

On the South Rim

Everybody needs beauty as well as bread,
places to play in and pray in, where nature may heal
and give strength to body and soul.

—JOHN MUIR

"I want you to start thinking about a medical retirement," the doctor said to me after examining the last batch of x-rays. "I don't know why that foot is not healing, but it isn't."

It had been several long months since I broke my left foot, and I had done everything he had prescribed. I had used the crutches, done the electrical therapy, soaked it, wrapped it, babied it, and spent weeks upon weeks hobbling around in a special boot. Nothing seemed to help.

In all of my life I had never come close to being so vexed by a physical ailment or injury. All over a misplaced step at the end of an evening shift, scrambling through a residential front yard while responding to a possible neighborhood break-in. I never saw that low curb in the darkness in front of me, and it most likely wouldn't have even slowed me down had I been in street clothes.

But weighed down with full DPS uniform, soft body armor, gun, back-up gun, spare ammunition, handheld radio, handcuffs, and wearing thin-soled western ropers, it was simply too much pressure for that one bone to withstand. I distinctly heard it go "pop," felt the pain, and lost all interest in running down any possible bad guys in the near vicinity.

Providentially enough, the injury occurred at the end of my shift, so I left the patrol car at my partner's residence and limped

The Window from the Pinnacles Trail

home a couple of blocks away. Hoping against all hope, next morning I tried to stand on the foot and was rewarded with some real physical discomfort along with the sinking sensation that something was indeed seriously wrong.

I still suited up, managing to the get my left foot into that Justin boot, and checked in as being on duty when my partner showed up with the car. We had an area meeting that day in Sonora, so we drove over and I told Sgt. Mayfield I thought my foot had been broken the night before on patrol.

Carl Mayfield was not only my boss but as good a man as I ever stood shoulder to shoulder with. With a well-used face and blue eyes that could either warm or intimidate depending upon a smile or a steady stare, he was not the type to speak of words such as honor, courage, and commitment; he lived them. This carried over into his profession as a highway patrol sergeant, a first sergeant in the Marine Corps Reserve, and as both a husband and a father. None of us knew it at the time, but little more than a year later cancer would accomplish what neither Iraqi bullets nor car wrecks nor any criminal could ever do: it would take his life and leave me one short of that special cadre of men whom I was proud to call "friend."

Now Carl didn't want to hear about my left foot for numerous reasons, including the heaping mounds of paperwork involved when reporting such an incident. If there is one thing the Texas Department of Public Safety is big on, it's paperwork. In this case, reams and reams of it detailing every tiny aspect as to what had transpired. And just when you thought you were finished with it, someone up the chain of command either loses some or gets the happy idea they want still more for their own files. Bureaucracies should be rationed paper at all times; it would alleviate a lot of mischief by the desk-bound.

When I first contacted my assigned orthopedic specialist in San Angelo, he had been quite optimistic. The bone running on the outside part of my foot was fractured lengthways, yet he was certain it would start healing within a month or so. Now, some seven months later, he had gone way to the negative side in his outlook, while some of my own worst fears were coming to fruition. Every man wants to leave his profession with his integrity and health intact, especially as a peace officer. I had less than three years left before I was set to pull the pin, and then this happened.

The doctor continued to ruminate over my present condition, saying that in hindsight he probably should have done surgery immediately and installed some screws. But that was then, and the way it was now the foot would never be the same. I wouldn't be able to do much with it even if it healed in the future. Then he started talking about things like arthritis and osteoporosis settling in. I didn't hear much more beyond that, as I was doing my own thinking. Okay Ollie, this is another fine mess you've gotten yourself into. I did hear him say we could wait until the next scheduled appointment, however, before we began the disability process. That was the one lifeline left; made up of coils that would last little more than another month.

I drove back to Ozona and sat down with my wife Cathy, telling her of all the high points in my conversation with the doctor. But in this particular circumstance, it was all of the low ones. Both of us had been praying faithfully for my recovery, as had a lot of other folks whom I would never be able to adequately thank for their concern and many kindnesses. Through it all the two people who had hung with me the tightest were our sons Levi and Ethan. They were both in high school and very busy in so many different ways, yet both had turned to and picked up a lot of slack since the old man had been crippled up.

That night after the doctor's visit I lay there in bed considering what my next step should be, literally and otherwise. I still had my faith and knew in my heart that God does work in miraculous ways. I also knew He had a plan for each of us, although we usually don't have a clue as to what it might be. As I stared into the blackness and the hours ticked by, that faith collided headlong with the lingering doubts, concerns, and harsh realities numbering themselves before me.

Don't ask me exactly how it happened, but during this solitary time of soul-searching and questions, a thought came in the wee hours of the morning. Scratch that; it was more like something reached deep inside and posited a primal need that had been lingering on the sidelines for all those months before. I had to get back to where I had come from, a place that, no matter how bad things might be, still managed to provide a special solace not to be had anyplace else. I needed to pack up my many troubles and strike out for the Big Bend.

For as long as I could remember, the Big Bend had often been my refuge when confronting the adversities each of us face in our individual lives. It had served as a frequent source for inspiration, a safe harbor where I could go and heal when the hurting got too bad. I hadn't been there in a year, as the therapy for my foot had taken priority over most of my other activities. Besides, why go when you can't walk through those great expanses and truly experience the very essence of what it was? Well, it was high time to do so, and in an inexplicable way I felt that an answer for my broken foot would reveal itself in the process.

Two weeks later I was standing in the Chisos Basin, looking at the head of the South Rim Trail and making certain the laces for my left boot were lashed extra tight. Cathy and our two sons looked on somewhat apprehensively, and both Levi and Ethan offered to carry my hiking gear. No thanks, though it was a kind offer and appreciated. I shouldered my harness and started up the path, albeit at a slower pace than I could ever recall using.

It was early in the morning as we began our ascent; I would need all of the daylight hours available to make the circuit on today's agenda. The air was crisp with the promise of a new day, filling me with the urge to move out in a manner that the foot simply could not support. So I had to content myself with just being here, crippling along as I gingerly picked out my steps in the heavy, steel-shanked boots.

But other than an occasional protest from the fractured bone, there was something to be said about being forced to use such a leisurely pace. I had made this hike several times before, yet now I was being constrained to a speed that allowed me to better enjoy the beauty nature had seen fit to place all around. To put a slight bend to an old adage, sometimes the journey brings as much to the eye as the destination itself.

Long before there was a national park this basin was known as Green Gulch. A roughly triangular piece of terrain some two-and-a-half miles long and about a mile-and-a-half wide at its eastern base, it slopes off to the west through a series of rolling rises and ravines that gather together to drain through Oak Canyon and what is known as the Window.

Many consider the Chisos Basin to be the most beautiful spot in Texas easily accessible by vehicle, and the National Park Service takes great pains to display this crown jewel of the Big Bend. At some 5,500 feet in elevation at the visitor's center, it is also one of the highest points in the Lone Star State that can be driven to by paved road. Much of the park's 1,200 species of plants, as well as its wide variety of birds and mammals, can be found here or among the craggy mountain peaks jutting thousands of feet above in every direction. If the Chisos Mountains are an isolated bastion of vitality and life not found elsewhere in the vastness of the Chihuahuan Desert, then this basin serves as its beating heart.

On the more modern topographical maps Green Gulch is still listed, but it now refers to the canyon you drive through before entering the Basin itself. This name change is not unique; when the National Park Service took over, several places and landmarks underwent this for one reason or another. Yet this has been the way of the Big Bend as far back as recorded documents can take us. The land itself remains, but man's marks and references to it prove constant in change.

At a little over a mile up the Laguna Meadow Trail, the gentle ups and downs in elevation play out, and you begin to climb in earnest. This difference called for even more attention to how I placed my left boot, and where. Though the foot had been injured for over half a year, my legs were still in pretty good shape by reason of riding a recumbent bike over the past few months. Besides, at this clip I could have probably crawled along quite nicely.

Oh, but the sights that present themselves when easing through the Chisos at such an unhurried gait. It was early summertime, and a recent rain had sprouted a hundred shades of green against a multitude of contrasting colors reflecting from the rocks, soil, and sky. These mountains are a very special place, and the loop to the South Rim affords the sojourner the opportunity to truly experience why. Many hiking and backpacking blogs and periodicals refer to this trail as one of the most scenic to be found in the state of Texas. Others go further and compare it favorably to some of the best known in the nation, stating that you can't even call yourself a hiker until you have gone to the South Rim of the Chisos.

As the contour lines tighten, the trail begins zigzagging back and forth as it negotiates the steepening incline. The crisp feeling of early morning dissipates rapidly as the sun rises higher in the sky, basking you in warmth where the path peeks out from the overhanging canopy of trees, boulders, and canyon walls. Through gaps in the foliage you occasionally catch glimpses of Casa Grande Peak to the northeast. Directly to your east sits Toll Mountain, while Emory Peak, the highest point in the Chisos, looms before you to the south. Ultimately the route to the South Rim will circumnavigate the southwestern base of Emory Peak. By the time you make the turnoff to the Laguna Meadow campsites, you might think you have already done some climbing. Just remember, the peak itself is another thousand feet above this trail, and toward the top on this side it runs mostly straight up.

Emory Peak is named after William Hemsley Emory, one of those great pioneering Americans whom history has mostly overlooked with the passage of time. A West Point graduate, William H. Emory was a man blessed with many different talents and abilities. Throughout his eventful life, he put that multitude of talents and abilities to their utmost use on many occasions. Emory had an exquisite eye for detail and was known as one of the foremost cartographers of his era. Unerringly accurate in his mapping, Emory served his country ably as a commissioner in the survey of this portion of the Big Bend in 1852. He was also instrumental in the cartographical work done for the Treaty of Guadalupe Hidalgo, the Gadsen Purchase, and in establishing the American-Canadian borderline.

Yet William Emory was not only an exceptional surveyor; he was also a keen student of the botanical, animal, and human life he encountered during his many travels along the frontiers of

Casa Grande Mountain from Laguna Meadow Trail

our nation. This professional army officer kept exacting notes of his many observations, including those made of the customs and culture of the Native Americans he came into contact with while serving his country. Over time, Emory became known as something of an authority on certain Indian tribes.

His decades as an officer in the United States Army proved him to be a man of excellent discernment who possessed great personal courage. During the trying days following the fall of Fort Sumter, then-Colonel Emory was in command of an isolated Union Army detachment located in present-day Oklahoma, just north of the Red River. Cut off by a far more numerous Confederate force and exposed to their continuous probing actions, Emory staged an impressive breakout with the assistance of the renowned Lenape warrior and scout Black Beaver. During his march toward friendly lines across the eastern part of what was then known as the Indian Territories, this intrepid West Point graduate not only took his command to Fort Leavenworth intact but also managed to take some of the first Confederate prisoners of the war.

Now in his mid-fifties, Emory continued to serve with great distinction during the Shenandoah Valley campaign and ultimately held the rank of Major General in the Union Army. Some twenty years later, following Lee's surrender at Appomattox, William H. Emory died at the age of 76 and was entombed at the Congressional Cemetery in Washington, DC. So the next time you look up at that mountain, think of the man it was named after, a rare breed well worth riding the river with.

As you get closer to Emory Peak, the switchbacks cease and you come through a pass that serves as a favored resting spot for many who take this route. Here you can wander around or sit on a crude wooden bench emplaced decades ago and take a breather. From this spot you can see back into the Basin itself, giving the opportunity to figure how far and how high you have already come. For those who need an even better view, there is a small trail that leads up a steep little knoll situated just to the west. This was one occasion I didn't elect to climb this hill, thinking it better just to kick back and give the foot a short respite.

In truth I had little choice in the matter, as Cathy and my two sons were insistent about taking the break. I think they were far more concerned than I was regarding my present circumstance. All in all I was feeling pretty fit; it was invigorating to be out here and moving around on my own two feet, no matter how slowly. Though the trail can be steep in certain sections, both routes to the South Rim are well-defined and laid out, with very few of the challenges found on many of the other paths in this park. I also had the added benefit of the steel shanks embedded in my tactical boots, which combined with thick socks and like soles helped support and cushion the foot. Barring a really stupid move on my part, it would be more than good to go the entire distance.

Following the short interlude at the pass we pushed on at my leisurely pace, although I was making better time now as the abrupt elevation changes were behind us. We hiked past the markers for the Laguna Meadow campsites, continuing past the Blue Creek Trail connection and on toward Colima Trail turnoff. If one wants to make an extended backpacking trip along this route there are numerous primitive camping spots scattered along the way, though some may be temporarily closed for one reason or another. A quick check with the park service will give you the latest information on these.

Our little party stopped numerous times en route to the South Rim. The reason wasn't so much in needing a short repose as the desire to take a moment to embrace the captivating views that transformed and reorganized at most every other step. To the left was Emory Peak, soaring above us at an elevation of 7,825 feet. To the right was the massive cut that makes up Blue Creek Canyon, providing the watershed for the creek bed far below snaking past Carousel Mountain and then west beyond Castolon, before finally feeding into the Rio Grande some fifteen miles away. From this vantage point, you can see it coursing nearly all the way down to the river.

The surrounding scenery isn't limited to the opposing landmarks of Emory Peak and Blue Creek Canyon, either. From the trail you can also take in Goat Mountain, Anguila Mesa, Cerro Castellan, and numerous other sierras and peaks both near and far, stretching all the way into northern Mexico. There is also the Rio Grande River itself, the lush banks of green visible up to the mouth of Santa Elena Canyon. As you get closer to the rim the raw, natural beauty of this rough-and-tumble country only becomes more apparent and spectacular.

If a hiker wants to take a shorter circuit, you can use Colima Trail as a turnaround point back to the Basin. It links up with Boot Canyon Trail, which ultimately becomes the Pinnacles as it winds back down below. Some do this to afford themselves the opportunity to climb Emory Peak itself, which is accessed by a spur that branches off west near the summit of the Pinnacles route. My foot was still game and so was I, so we ignored the shorter loop and kept on for the South Rim.

There is one matter that requires strong emphasis at this juncture, and is applicable to any time you are negotiating the Chisos Mountains trails complex. Though some of these paths can run within a couple of hundred yards of each other on occasion, as seen on a map, one should not be tempted to simply cut across in an attempt to save time or cut distance. The intervening terrain is often a lot tougher going than it might first appear to the inexperienced eye.

This is tricky, unforgiving country with steep ravines, bluffs, unstable slides, and dozens of other hidden pitfalls piled one atop the other. If you are unfortunate enough to get hurt up here or lost, it may be a long while before anyone finds you—and longer still before they can get you any help. People have died in the Big Bend National Park, usually because they overestimated their personal abilities and underestimated this demanding environment. So do yourself a favor and stick to the routes laid out; it just works out better for everyone involved.

Lost Mine Peak through Boot Canyon

Furthermore, when you come upon those sections where the trail zigzags through abrupt elevation changes, stay on the marked track. These trails see a lot of use, and those switchbacks not only help negotiate the steeper parts but also keep erosion at bay. When you cleave your way straight through to save a couple of steps, you are aiding and abetting that erosion. This is an ongoing problem, and the park service has specifically constructed these trails so that future generations can enjoy this magnificent land as much as we do. If you are so lazy or pressed for time as to not show a little deserved respect for this grand example of God's handiwork, do these old mountains a real service and just stay home.

About a half mile past the Colima Trail turnoff the route mostly levels out, and you circle around the back slope of the rim, affording you the opportunity to look across the top of the Chisos Mountain Range to the northeast. You peer through Boot Canyon as if it were a rear v-shaped rifle sight while the summit of Lost Mine Peak serves as a front sight post. The peak is a prominent landmark, and this location allows you to see the top of it from a fairly unique perspective. It's another good spot to take a quick break and admire the view before you.

From this spot it is less than a mile to the South Rim itself, making for an easy walk because all of the climbing is now behind you. Meandering along, you continue to see trees and vegetation one could never imagine finding in the middle of the parched, unrelenting Chihuahuan Desert. It is almost a surreal impression for those who have an intimate knowledge of the hard country that surrounds this uplifted refuge. Some have remarked that the Chisos range is much like a mountainous island harboring animal and plant species that could not survive in the surrounding oceans of cacti, mesquite, and moisture-starved soil. I cannot think of a better analogy.

You are almost upon the South Rim before you know it, walking slightly upwards until the trees part and the blue sky falls away to a horizon that now seems strangely below you. I have been here several times before, yet on each occasion I have to stop and gape in wonder at what opens up before me. The word *beautiful* should be used sparingly in one's language, as it and the word *love* get overworked and undervalued far too much in everyday conversation. But to me this is one of the most stunningly beautiful sights I have ever laid my eyes upon.

It also tends to make one feel mighty small and insignificant, and presents the kind of circumstance in nature that forces you to come to grips with that insignificance on a purely individual basis. The four of us fanned out to take in the sheer enormity of the panorama before us, not saying a word for fear of spoiling the moment for the other three. The sky was blue, the sun was shining, and a southern breeze was sending hawks, eagles, and other large birds soaring both above and below us, catching the wind currents along the massive bluffs and pirouetting in the graceful manner that only these royalties of the air seem to possess. If you do not feel intimately alive at such a moment, then for all useful purposes you can best be categorized as clinically dead.

While letting this all soak in, I found a likely place to sit down and prop my foot up. It had carried me nearly seven miles to get to this spot, and that victory deserved a hard-won rest. I looked over to Cathy, who had never been up to the South Rim. She was smiling with eyes dancing in wonderment and joy, her face basking in the glory of the breathtaking scenery displayed before us. Someone once said that a life is not made up of days or years, but of moments. This was one of those moments.

Since we were about to our halfway point and getting hungry, we elected to take our nooning here. Using our laps and the

The South Rim

surrounding rocks for our dinner tables; we sat and dined as a spectacular world of color, shadow, and substance enveloped us, entertaining not only our eyes but also our spirits. It was as if a person could spend an entire life here and never fully follow or comprehend what was constantly happening around them.

After finishing our meal we knew we had to move on, so we saddled up and threaded our way easterly along the vertical periphery, taking in the magnificent views from at least a hundred different angles. When we came upon the intersection for the trail that runs through Boot Canyon, a decision was called for: take the shorter route through this crevice or push on the extra mile or so that makes up the Northeast Rim Trail.

We had sufficient time, and the weather was as favorable as we could hope for. My foot was letting me know that it was being pushed, yet nothing on the discomfort scale where another mile and a half of easy walking would make much difference. But most importantly, Cathy had never been to the Northeast Rim either, and who knew if she would have the chance again to do so. We steered on to the longer route.

Through here the path travels as close to the rim as safety and good sense allows, maximizing the opportunity to experience numerous broad vistas to your south. This section continues on for about a mile until reaching a tip on this towering escarpment known as the Northeast Rim. From here one is rewarded with another incredible view that sweeps from Crown Mountain and Lost Mine Peak all the way over to the craggy uplifts west of Dominguez Mountain.

From the overlook on the Northeast Rim, the track swings back around and meanders toward the west until it drops into and deadends at Boot Canyon Trail. Inside this picturesque cut is one of the prettiest walks to be found in the park, and you will be inclined to think you are in some of the higher country of Colorado or Utah rather than in West Texas, within a dozen air miles or so of Mexico. There are abundant oak, piñon pine, and juniper trees along the way, as well as what is reportedly the only native stand of Arizona cypress in the Lone Star State.

There is also water usually present, fed by springs and run-offs that collect inside the canyon. As you work your way down the deepening chasm, the signs of water become more prevalent. During certain seasons and years there can be quite a bit of it, at least for this country. A small stream runs intermittently from pool to pool toward the waiting Juniper Canyon, where it disappears again somewhere on its journey. But like other natural water sources in the Big Bend, you should not count on it as your sole supplier during a hike or backpacking trip. It has been known to be bone dry, too.

Along this route is a bit of man-made history. As you near the location where Colima Trail links up with Boot Canyon, you will come across a shingled cabin and some metal corrals. Some fifty years ago this small, isolated structure was a seasonal ranger station. From here park rangers patrolled the trail network for this part of the Chisos Mountains, usually on horseback. During that time it was still possible for tourists to take trail rides up from the Basin, and the cabin and corrals also served as a layover point for them. Tragically, some decades ago a young woman was fatally injured near here on one of those rides. The cabin still serves as an occasional shelter for park employees when in the area, or for other personnel engaged in some sort of officially sanctioned work.

Past the cabin you begin to climb out on the west side of the canyon, which allows you to get a good look at the landmark that gave Boot Canyon its name. Situated on the opposing side of the cut, this solitary tower of bare stone stands some fifty feet high

The 'boot' in Boot Canyon

and from many angles looks like an upside down, high-top western boot. The track takes you fairly close to the pillar before it veers away northwesterly toward Emory Peak and the Pinnacles.

Upon reaching the pass above the Pinnacles you begin descending back into the Basin in earnest. Two other things happen here as far as routes go, Boot Canyon Trail becomes Pinnacles Trail while a spur takes off west, leading to the top of Emory Peak. This path is about a mile in length and makes for a fairly steep, rocky scramble near the summit. A couple of summers ago, my sons and I went from the Basin to the top of Emory Peak in well under two hours. With a broken foot I would not be trying to best that record today, nor was I keen on that last three hundred yards to the top, so we passed it by.

The Pinnacles is named after the large, upright columns of solid rock that line the western side of Toll Mountain. The Pinnacles Trail threads its way through the southernmost part of these natural stone pillars, offering striking views and memorable vistas in its own right. The route drops quickly in altitude by way of a series of switchbacks, allowing you ample opportunity to study the impressive rock formations both above and around you, as well as the area making up the Chisos Basin below. Like Laguna Meadow Trail and the others in this particular system, the pathway is well-defined and cared for.

The long shadows of late evening were setting the scene for oncoming nightfall when we finally trudged back into the Basin complex. That left foot was really starting to protest against anything more than it had already been put through, and I was looking forward to a comfortable place to drop my gear. Tired, sweaty, hot, and hungry we made our way to our lodging and plopped down on the nearest suitable piece of furniture. Gingerly I untied my laces and with some trepidation eased the injured foot out of the tactical boot. All things considered, it looked pretty good, and after some time on a footstool began feeling even better.

Levi and Ethan broke out their topographical maps and did some figuring, coming to the conclusion that we had covered close to fourteen and a half miles on our South Rim jaunt. That was about the same distance noted in the park information booklets, and good enough work for a couple of teenagers still in high school. Then they were in their running gear and out the door again, already in training for their upcoming cross-country season starting in the fall. The vigor and restlessness of youth, you might say.

Sitting in that cushioned chair I looked over at my wife, who had also taken a well deserved seat nearby.

"Thanks for going, Sweetheart. I'm sorry I held the rest of you up; the boys won't get much of a run before dark."

"Don't worry about them, they have plenty of time to make it up before the season starts." She leaned forward, smiling at me; "Besides, it's the only time I have ever had to wait on you rather than you guys wait on me."

I smiled back and shifted the foot to a different position.

"How's the foot?" she asked apprehensively.

"Passable," I replied. "It'll be better after a good night's sleep."

"I sure hope you know what you're doing," she cautioned. "That doctor in San Angelo would probably have a cow if he knew about this."

"Well, I did everything he wanted and look at where I am. You just gotta stick with me on this one, Mrs. English."

She looked me square in the eye, her inner steel peeking out from beneath the silken glove. "I always have, Mr. English, and don't you forget it."

We spent the next few days mostly traveling by vehicle and taking short, easy walks around Santa Elena Canyon, Tuff Canyon, Glenn Spring, and Dog Canyon before heading back to Ozona. Meanwhile the foot felt, well, *different.* It didn't hurt as much, hardly swelled, and felt like it was growing stronger all the while. It also had a strange tingling sensation around the fractured part of the bone, as if something was happening inside.

Some two weeks later I was back in the doctor's office again, having the foot examined. As had become routine, they first took the monthly x-rays and then had me wait in one of those little examination rooms until the doctor could see me. Some minutes later he burst through the door, waving the x-rays around in his hand and with a great big grin on his face.

"Mr. English," he said excitedly, "I don't know what happened or what you have been doing, but that foot is finally starting to heal!" He clipped the x-rays to a wall-mounted illuminator box and turned on its light. "Take a look for yourself!"

I got in close, put on my reading glasses, and studied the x-rays as best a layman could. Sure enough, you could see where the crack running lengthwise through the bone was beginning to fill in. The specialist also pointed it out for me for good measure, and began singing my praises for sticking it out and not pushing for a disability settlement earlier. For myself, I gave my praises to the Good Lord above when it came to this little miracle.

Yet according to my specialist, the battle was far from over. Even if the bone was to completely heal I was cautioned about not getting my hopes up too high. Knowing I was a physically active person, he warned me that the foot would probably never be close to what it was before the injury. He went on to explain the high probabilities of osteoporosis and/or arthritis that would never totally go away. I listened to what the man had to say, but I still had my money on the Lord and the healing effects of the Big Bend.

Three months later, the evening of October 31 marked my return to patrol duty. I had been working that left foot as hard as I dared, and it was coming around fast. The aching and weakness were going away, and the foot no longer had that shrunken appearance. For my coworkers, the irony of my being put back into a black-and-white on Halloween Night was not lost upon anyone.

Slightly more than a month following I was standing on a track surface in San Angelo, waiting to begin the running portion of my Physical Assessment Test for the DPS. There was a forty-mile-an-hour norther blowing in, one of those Panhandle fronts carrying along half of Lubbock in the form of an enormous red dust cloud that nearly blotted out the sun. My physical assessment observers had made it clear they thought I was nuts for trying this so soon and on such a miserable day; I made it clear that I was way past the point of wanting off their walking wounded list. I got the signal to start.

When I crossed the finish line some minutes later, the stopwatch said I had aced the course. I also managed to max everything else other than the vertical jump, where I only posted a 90% rating. My left foot was still not quite back up to speed for that sort of thing, but then again I wasn't hanging around many basketball courts while on patrol.

However, one other hurdle presented itself almost immediately afterwards. One of the obvious reasons I broke the foot in the first place was the type of boot we were forced to wear on duty. Admittedly, black ropers look sharp in a western-cut uniform, but are lousy for most anything else other than casual walking or on a dance floor. Since returning to full duty, I had started wearing highly-polished Bates tactical boots to keep the same injury from happening all over again.

That lasted about as long as it took for certain DPS supervisors to get wind of my little insurrection. At first I tried to argue commonsensically with them about my footwear needs, and the reasons for them. A word to the wise, if you will. There are two kinds of people in this world who are put in charge of other people: those who are leaders and those who are supervisors. The bigger the bureaucracy and the more top-heavy the organization, the more the supervisors and the fewer the leaders. The Texas Department of Public Safety is really big into bureaucracies and being top-heavy.

Rather than waste my breath I went back to my orthopedic specialist and explained what was going on. The doctor was more than slightly chagrined and immediately submitted medical documents on my behalf that supported my wearing of tactical boots. He also stated that he hoped the DPS challenged him on it.

They didn't. This was not my first battle with certain supervisors in the DPS, and it wouldn't be my last, even at this late stage of the game. By the time I retired, I figured I had a good enough win/loss ratio as to make most football coaches envious. After becoming a first-class citizen again—i.e. a civilian—I was told

The South Rim with the Sierra Quemada below

that some of those same supervisors had named ulcers after me. I sure hope so.

It's been nearly ten years since I broke that left foot. Sometimes when it gets cold and wet it acts a little funky, but that could be a result of advancing age as much as anything else. I look back now and count my many blessings that came out of this episode. Doctors by nature are pessimists when it comes to physical injuries and general health, particularly when the healing process starts out so badly. Nevertheless, that specialist had been more than adamant about my considering a medical disability and later about the foot giving me real problems in the future.

But so far it hasn't, and I give thanks to a benevolent God for that fact. I also give some credit to those special places He created; those places where I can go and, to quote Muir, "play in and pray in, where nature may heal and give strength to body and soul." Don't ask me how it works that way, it just does. At least for me.

And for as long as the Good Lord sees fit to give me life, I will continue to return to that special place of mine known as the Big Bend.

CHAPTER 10

North of Lajitas

You cannot help but learn more as you take the world into your hands. Take it up reverently, for it is an old piece of clay, with millions of thumbprints on it.

—JOHN UPDIKE

It does not seem so long ago that when one set foot in Lajitas, Texas, there was the distinct sense of standing on ground made from a mishmash of Boquillas flagstone, loamy soil, lore, legend, and history. This feeling is harder to imagine these days, as you have to see past the golf courses, pro shops, "Hollywood Western" buildings, wine and cheese bazaars, condominiums, and other assorted high-dollar tourist attractions that have mostly obliterated what was once here, and why. It is a desecration not only in a physical sense, but also in the general bastardization of a way of life now mostly ignored or forgotten.

But the ghosts of the past still speak out, if you listen with your heart and mind beyond what too much civilization has done here. Lajitas has seen Comanche, Spaniard, Apache, Mexican, Texican, *Norteamericano,* scalp hunter, soldier, mercenary, bandit, hero, killer, cowboy, farmer, miner, smuggler, revolutionary, dreamer, and many a pragmatic realist pass through its environs. Each had his own story, and each had his own reason for being here, if not for any longer than to take a lay of the land before crossing the river running below.

That men of widely varying backgrounds would be drawn to such a place was inevitable. Though the name Lajitas is fairly recent, the locale itself has been of regional note for as long as humankind has traveled through this area. The site sits on a low bluff overlooking the Rio Grande, a safe height above a river

Lajitas Mesa from the Old Military Road

that can turn from a meandering, muddy stream into a torrent of rushing water when the rains come to the desert. If one is familiar with how the Rio Grande runs through this part of the country, one can better appreciate this wide, sweeping space with irrigable land seemingly out of place among so many miles of rocky canyons and narrow passageways. At the foot of the low bluffs is what was considered the best natural ford between Del Rio and El Paso, formed by the same flat rock slabs that litter the area and give Lajitas its name. The word translates roughly into "little flat stones."

Some say that Cabeza de Vaca crossed here in 1530, but that is highly debatable. However, documents do state that Spanish explorer Antonio de Espejo almost certainly did in 1588. As time passed and Indian tribes such as the Comanche and the Apache acclimated themselves to the horse, it became a major crossing and favored meeting area for the marauding bands as they forced other, more peaceful tribes out of the region.

These bloody raids and attacks were later targeted against Spanish citizens, leading New Spain to establish a series of presidios in the mid-1770s. A number of these outposts were strung through this inhospitable land they called *El Despoblado*, including the one at San Carlos some ten air miles south of Lajitas. The effort was doomed to failure given the lack of available military resources, not to mention the will to persevere, and the Indian attacks continued mostly unabated. The early Spanish and then Mexican settlers, along with the more peaceful Indian bands, were mostly left with three choices: move on, strike some sort of accommodation with the fierce hostiles, or die.

These were the forced circumstances for many decades: years of hard living eked out of the Chihuahuan Desert, punctuated by sudden butchery and death. Another dynamic was added to this highly volatile mixture with the arrival of Anglo-Americans during the Mexican War, who were pushing the warlike tribes farther into the southwest region of modern-day Texas. Some of these new arrivals brought their own savagery and brand of bloodletting, and that list would surely include a certain John Joel Glanton.

During the infant years of the Texas Republic, outsized, larger-than-life men represented both saint and sinner, patriot and villain in this vast, untamed land. One of these was a youngster who originally hailed from South Carolina, and who is said to have first been a ranger at the age of sixteen. He was also one of the most controversial and star-crossed characters to ever step upon the Lone Star stage. Throughout his short, violent life, Glanton was involved in numerous bloodlettings and killings on both sides of the law. He repeatedly weaved across the societal lines separating good from bad, and was said at one time to have been banished from Texas entirely, by none other than Sam Houston himself.

A man of some intelligence and an engaging personality, Glanton was rumored to have lost his bride-to-be to a Lipan Apache tomahawk just days before he was to be married. From that point forward he became a well-known Indian hater, a central part of his psyche that remained true in what was to follow. This budding harbinger of death proved utterly fearless in personal combat, serving with distinction as a Texas Ranger during both the Texas Revolution and the Mexican-American War. That is, until he reportedly murdered a Mexican civilian, which led to an arrest warrant issued by the Army. But the wily Glanton managed to evade the military authorities, joining up with yet another ranger unit and fighting to the end of the conflict. He returned to Texas as a minor war hero.

After the war, the "hero" veneer quickly lost its luster, and there emerged the reality of an ugly soul bent upon obtaining money by whatever means necessary. While seeking a more fertile environment to channel these dark urges, he ventured into the wilderness of the Trans Pecos region at the head of what was called the Glanton Gang. Soon enough he and his cohorts were involved in the vicious business of collecting Apache scalps for bounty paid by the Chihuahuan government. When hostile scalps proved too difficult to obtain, he and his band turned to the hair of peaceful Indians as well as unlucky Mexican citizens caught unawares.

The gang's rampages included a reported mass slaughter along the lower reaches of Terlingua Creek, near the mouth of Santa Elena Canyon. Glanton and his band of cutthroats utilized the river ford at Lajitas, then called Comanche Crossing or San Carlos Crossing, numerous times during their depredations. This continued until the citizens of Chihuahua caught on to what was happening, forcing the scalphunters to abandon the Big Bend country forever. Ultimately Glanton and most of his gang met a well-deserved demise in April of 1850 at the hands of Yuma Indians in Southern Arizona. John Joel Glanton died at thirty-one years old.

In 1852 the Lajitas area was visited by the Chandler Expedition, part of an international boundary commission mapping out the region following the end of the Mexican-American war. The military contingent was commanded by Second Lieutenant Duff C. Green, United States Army. In his field notes Green referred to the future Lajitas site as "Comanche Pass." He also made mention of the wide, well-beaten paths crossing the river, proof positive of its storied use by Spaniards, Mexicans, and Indians, and, most notoriously of all, as one of the main routes for the great Comanche War Trail into Old Mexico.

While in the vicinity Green came upon the Comanche chief Mano making his own way across the Rio Grande. The two armed parties spent some time sizing each other up before deciding to enter into a guarded parley. Mano claimed that he had been at peace with the United States of America for over a year, and was simply taking his people down to Durango. The two exchanged gifts, the lieutenant giving the chief a steer for butchering and Mano reciprocating with a fine horse for the Army officer. It wasn't until later that Green learned that Mano and his band had killed four *norteamericanos* on the El Paso to San

Antonio Road, and had been en route to Mexico with their ill-gotten loot. Most likely the horse Green received from the chief was part of the haul from that attack. Never let it be said that the Comanche did not possess a fine sense of irony and humor.

It was in the middle of summer of 1860 when Lieutenant William H. Echols of the US Army Camel Corps arrived at what he called San Carlos Crossing. The lieutenant and his famous camels had departed San Antonio some three months prior, traveling west across the Pecos River to Fort Davis and down to present-day Presidio and Fort Leaton. The next phase of his march was to reconnoiter the lower parts of the mostly unexplored Big Bend.

In his official diary first mention is found of the word *Lahita,* the logical spelling for a Spanish derived word by an Anglo hand. Lieutenant Echols and his camels had battled their way from Fort Leaton across to the *Lates Lengua,* now known as Terlingua Creek, and down to the crossing via the western branch of the Comanche Trail. It was a route deemed nigh impassable by others who had advised him not to even try.

Intent on finding a navigable track to what he called the San Carlos Road, Echols nevertheless pushed on. By the time he had reached present day Lajitas, the young officer was in full agreement with the prior warnings he had received from the locals around Fort Leaton. Condemning most of the improvised route as being unfit for either man or beast, he complained bitterly about the heretofore unimaginably brutal going through a maze of broken canyons cutting across the jagged, rock-strewn terrain. Concerning one stretch he wrote that it was "the most rugged, roughest, most tortuous and cragged" land he had ever seen, and until now could have never conceived that such country existed. The good lieutenant would not be the last newcomer to the Big Bend to form such an opinion.

As the years went by, the mortal threat posed by the appearance of the Comanche Moon became little more than the stuff of memory and lore. But Lajitas Crossing, or whatever other name one chose to call it, was still being utilized by a wide assortment of characters involved in both legal and illegal activities. For the enterprising sort, smuggling has always been a lucrative undertaking in the Big Bend, be it liquor, guns, drugs, livestock, candelilla wax, or human captives. Whatever the going currency in a given situation, this old crossing saw it all and more.

By the 1890s profitable mines such as the Marfa and Mariposa were pulling cinnabar ore out of the ground, and millionaires were being made in the process. Families from both sides of the border flocked to the area looking for a better way of life, and many settled around Lajitas Crossing on account of the fertile soil as well as the commerce sparked by the needs of miners with American dollars in their pockets.

Such a boon in economic activity on an international border was duly noted by the United States Government, and in 1900 Lajitas became a substation port of entry. A customs house was established, which in turn brought in even more families. By 1902 the community had a store, a saloon, and a combination Catholic Church and schoolhouse claiming some fifty students on the rolls.

Much of this growth was due to the determination of one man by the name of Howard Washington McGuirk, better known to all as H. W. The Arkansas native first came to the Big Bend in the mid-1880s and left a big enough legacy that area landmarks still bear his name. A man of many talents, he was a rancher, farmer, store owner, telephone lineman, mine manager, and Lajitas's leading citizen from about 1900 to 1917.

An Irish Catholic, McGuirk was instrumental in the building of the church/ schoolhouse that was constructed in 1901 with his money. The chosen schoolmaster was Professor Eugene Navarro, grandson of Jose Antonio Navarro, a noted patriot of the Texas Revolution. Professor Navarro was a well-regarded academic as well as a Confederate war veteran, having fought in several major engagements and twice being captured by Union forces. To assist in running the school the professor brought two of his daughters, Lucia and Josefa, to Lajitas as teachers. The latter would soon become Mrs. H. W. McGuirk, and their wedding was held in the same church McGuirk had built two years before.

Though Lajitas had been assigned a post office in 1901, it did not become operational until McGuirk petitioned for its opening with Josefa as postmaster in 1904. Ever the entrepreneur, he also bought and installed a large gasoline-powered water pump to better irrigate the farm fields between Lajitas proper and the mouth of Comanche Creek.

By 1910 the burning powder keg known as Mexico had finally detonated, followed by nearly twenty years of heartbreaking misery fed by revolution, famine, pestilence, raging epidemics, religious intolerance, mass executions, and wholesale murder.

Thousands upon thousands of refugees fled to Texas to escape the unending nightmare that had enveloped their native land. The fighting and dying swept through Northern Mexico like a fast-moving cancer, spurred on by ruthless principals whose all-consuming ambitions were coupled with little or no conscience in tempering them.

After the Villista attacks on Glenn Spring and other surrounding locales in early May of 1916, American troops arrived in force to protect the porous border of the Big Bend. Numerous army camps were established in the region, including one at Lajitas. Though it is often referred to as a cavalry post, infantry units were also stationed here during the height of the crisis.

When General Black Jack Pershing and his punitive expedition moved south in search of Pancho Villa, Lajitas with its venerable river crossing found itself of real tactical importance to the United States Army. The spur to Lajitas from the original mine road between Marfa and the Mariposa mines was upgraded and improved for logistical use, and local citizens began referring to it as the Military Road. It became the main thoroughfare from the area around Lajitas to the Army supply depot at Camp Marfa, later renamed Fort D. A. Russell.

Meanwhile H.W. McGuirk, worn by decades of hard work and closing in on seventy years old, moved to New Mexico after selling out to Thomas V. Skaggs in 1917—never to return. Skaggs, who had come to Lajitas as an itinerant Bible salesman, picked up the reins of local power and did what he could for the community in the years that followed. But it was Howard Washington McGuirk who came first and struggled most of all to keep Lajitas on the map of Texas. McGuirk left his name and his worldly legacy in the Big Bend, and some might suspect he also left part of his heart. This redoubtable pioneer lived only five more years after leaving Lajitas.

Within a few more years the military had left and the customs house shut down, while the area mines did much the same because of a glut in the cinnabar market following World War I. People went away to other places to live different lives, and Lajitas slowly began to collapse upon itself. As rock walls crumbled and adobe brick melted away, it became mostly known as a ghost town. The last hint of any spurt in growth occurred during the first days after the attack on Pearl Harbor, when a small detachment of Army troops was deployed to the old crossing. But less than a month later, they too were gone.

Nevertheless, a central relic from the border town's heyday not only continued to stand but also managed to do some mercantile business. By default, the Lajitas Trading Post was the only nearby source of goods, and it also served as a social meeting place for the remaining area denizens on both sides of the Rio Grande. Making a living as the proprietor of the store was not an easy task, though, and from the era of McGuirk and Skaggs forward the store passed from one owner to another. Then in 1949 Rex Ivey bought the place, along with much of the town site and surrounding acreage.

Ivey worked hard at making necessary repairs and improvements, including digging a water well and having an electrical power generator installed. But his wife Kitty made it abundantly clear that she was not going to live in such a god-awfully hot and isolated locale, especially with a veritable paradise like Alpine nearby to better suit her growing family's needs. I hardly know of any normal woman who would have faulted that logic.

So in 1961 my family moved to Lajitas, taking over the trading post under lease from Rex. Thus at two years old my education began in this new world on the front porch of that establishment, branching out in every direction to discover this strange, almost magical land that shaped and nurtured me through my growing years.

To even the most experienced traveler, the Big Bend often beguiles with its many contrasts and contradictions. Where one spot is as flat as the Panhandle plains, another situated a short distance away is as jagged and uneven as any terrain could ever be. For every place best described as a barren wasteland is often another hidden close by that harbors trees, green grass, and good water. One can be down on the river baking in blistering heat, while five miles away other folks might be complaining about a chill.

Several of the intriguing sights that set the Big Bend apart can be found by taking the remnants of the Military Road out of Lajitas. It guides past the east side of Lajitas Mesa and behind Contrabando Mountain, then drops into Fresno Canyon under the shadow of Wax Factory Laccolith. From there the road runs up the canyon between The Solitario and an impressive escarpment perched on the opposing side known as the Llano. Numerous massive arroyos formed along the eastern edge of this plateau, cutting their way down through the uplift and feeding into this broad-shouldered watershed. It is a rough, remote area, yet hidden jewels are to be found within that are well worth what it takes to get there.

These days most of this area belongs to the Big Bend Ranch State Park, but at that time it was private land belonging to the Big Bend Ranch Company. My family leased portions of the ranch's holdings along Fresno Canyon, as it was much easier for us to access this land from Lajitas than for the holders to come off the escarpment from their Saucedo headquarters. Our leased sections included much of Fresno Canyon from what was called Fresno Farm, situated along the Rio Grande, all the way up to the Smith Place.

Though the actual livestock work was done by horseback, we often traveled to the upper parts of our holdings by vehicle via what was left of the Military Road. After the army departed the Big Bend and the mines played out, the route fell into disuse, and by our time was only navigable from Lajitas to a bit north of the Smith Place. Bear in mind that passage had a lot to do with the weather; the last place you want to be is down in that canyon when Fresno Creek comes on a big rise.

For this purpose my grandmother had an International Scout, a vintage jeep-styled four-wheel drive with a small bed behind the removable cab. It was the closest thing you could get to a mountain goat on four tires and was her "wheeled weapon of choice" when headed for Fresno Canyon. She and I often partnered up in her trips back and forth when my grandfather was in that area working livestock. Papa used to say that if there ever were two yahoos up to no good, it was she and I in that Scout headed out for the far country.

It was in this manner I first got to know both that old road and the Fresno, peering at them through the dirty windshield of my grandmother's International Scout. As time went by I became big enough to spend a full day in the saddle alongside my grandfather and occasionally my father, increasing my budding knowledge of the surrounding country. The Fresno was my favorite place to be of any of our holdings, as everywhere you looked there seemed to be something that beckoned you to come and see.

Also, unlike many other parts of the Big Bend, there was not only water to be had, but good water. Numerous springs and waterholes dot many of the branches that feed into the chasm, and still more water can be found along the length of the creek itself. West of the canyon, the Llano's steep walls provide relief from the afternoon sun, as do stands of cottonwood trees strung out through the bottoms. There is nothing more pleasant on God's great earth than cool water and shade on a scorching summer day north of Lajitas.

When time came to work the Fresno my grandfather would sometimes overnight at the Smith Place, or near the ruins of a nineteenth-century ranch house known as the Madrid. But usually he would rise in the wee hours of the morning, making ready for the long day ahead while my grandmother fixed breakfast. It was a meal fit for royalty: eggs over easy, frijoles, tortillas, and fried venison steak washed down with cups of steaming-hot coffee. Even fifty years later I can think back to those pre-dawn breakfasts and start to salivate.

While we ate my grandparents would talk over their plans to meet somewhere in the canyon for lunch. When Papa was through he would finish getting his gear together while grandmother cleaned up and began thinking about a noon meal to feed him, along with any of the other hands who went along.

My grandfather would finish by loading his favorite horse, a big buckskin named Nylon, into the back of his GMC pickup. In those days many ranch trucks had what were called "cattle racks" mounted on them. These pen-like devices were fitted to the bed for carrying one or two horses in the back. You hardly ever see them around anymore, perhaps because no one makes real ranch trucks anymore. If you ever want to determine just how tough a pickup truck might be, try putting a thousand-pound ranch horse in it who might not want to be there and taking him someplace in the Big Bend.

There were a couple of different ways to access the canyon, and both my grandparents had their own particular favorites. The route my grandfather preferred started along the *El Camino del Rio* towards Presidio. Before reaching the old highway bridge at Fresno Creek, he would turn off to guide along the remains of Contrabando Road for a short distance before switching back toward the Fresno.

From that point forward it was one decaying, ancient trace of a track after another, with the judicious use of any available creek beds, before entering the Fresno itself near Wax Camp Laccolith. His way was certainly fastest of the available routes, as it made use of the highway for about the first six miles, and he never let any grass grow under that beat-up GMC. I do not believe I could recreate his exact route if I tried; Papa had a feel for terrain found in few other men and instinctively knew where and how to thread the needle. Meanwhile, Nylon would ride serenely along in the back, watching the world go by as that GMC banged and shuddered its way up the canyon. I can't say the same about anything or anyone else that accompanied him on those early morning sorties.

In contrast my grandmother's approach was far more measured and leisurely: she would finish cooking the noon meal, complete her other domestic chores, and load the Scout for the trip. Her favorite route was up the Military Road from Lajitas. She would quietly ease that International along, looking all about and studiously taking in her surroundings.

Some might make the wrong assumption when it came to her apparent abundance of caution. After all, that little four-wheel drive was far more capable off-road than Papa's GMC, especially when the truck had one or two horses in the back. But if you ever saw her in action, any notion that this petite, middle-aged lady was scared of anything or anybody would quickly be dispelled. Half Cherokee, half Irish, and all Texas ranch woman, she could hold her own with a vehicle, a horse, or a rifle against any and all comers.

The true reason for Granny's unhurried speed and direction was simple: it afforded the best opportunity to pick up some free venison along the way. Of course there was nothing wrong with the beef that we raised, but venison didn't cost us anything other than a well-placed bullet and the time spent dressing out a deer. It was a common routine for our family during those years, and my grandmother was about as crafty at this as anyone could be.

Originally, the Lajitas to Camp Marfa road ran much closer to the eastern side of Lajitas Mesa. Over the decades the road was cut and recut due to wear, washouts, or the need to run a feeder lane from the main way. My grandmother knew them all and had her favorite spots picked out, always careful never to "hunt out" a particular track or area. She would shoot one and then skillfully maneuver her International as close as possible to the dead animal. After that, the two of us would put the carcass into the bed of her little four-by-four. These were mule deer and usually a bit larger than an average white tail; sometimes the lift was a real struggle for a five-year-old kid and a woman who probably weighed 115 pounds sopping wet. But sooner or later we would get it done and be on the road again.

Once we met up with my grandfather, she'd let him know we had gotten a deer and that it needed dressing out. After lunch and before he took his afternoon siesta, Papa would haul the deer out and hang it from the nearest likely spot. Working deftly with his pocketknife, he'd mutter and complain about being married to a "durned old poacher." In return, Grandmother would admonish him for being a "straight-laced old maid," saying he never complained about poached venison being on the menu when he was hungry.

Of course during those years there was no game warden in the lower Big Bend that I ever saw. In fact, I was almost thirteen years old before I learned there was such a thing as a hunting season. Furthermore, there wasn't any kind of law present around Lajitas on a regular basis, other than an occasional border patrolman or Sheriff Williams driving down from Alpine on official business. Since the county seat was nearly a hundred miles away, the sheriff utilized my grandfather as a sort of special deputy, someone who could handle whatever came along until he could get there. With the only telephone in Lajitas being at the trading post or later inside my grandparents' separate residence, this made good sense in more ways than one.

Sometime after my grandfather passed away, I was home on leave and we were going through some of his personal things. There among the souvenirs of a man who had lived an arduous life and never asked any quarter from it was a badge. He had been a sheriff in his younger years, but this badge was different: it belonged to a game warden. I asked my grandmother about it and she replied; "Didn't you know? Your Papa was once a game warden back in the 1940s." It was only then the full meaning of their little inside joke became clear to me, and I found myself yet again wishing there had been more time to spend with this man who had meant so much to me. As you get older, time does become more precious. Especially the time you can never reclaim. Ultimately we would leave the Big Bend and the horizons of my world would broaden considerably, but on so many occasions my mind would wander back to that country north of Lajitas. The decades passed, and what had been private land came into the hands of the State of Texas, including much of that worn-out

Waterhole on western branch of Comanche Creek

road I had traveled when the world was younger and a thirty-mile round trip was often measured in terms of can-see to can't. I waited, sometimes not so patiently, for Texas Parks and Wildlife to open this area up to the public, anxious to return to the memories of my childhood. That waiting went on for years, and I found myself suspecting that some well-heeled politicians in Austin just might be using it for their own deer hunting, legal or not.

Nevertheless the day finally arrived, and my family and I checked into the Warnock Center, obtaining the necessary permits to take a hike up the old road. This visitor center is one of the more recent additions to Lajitas, and by far the most useful. Named after regional botanist and longtime Big Bend resident Barton Warnock, it not only serves as a check-in point for anyone wishing to enter the state park but also contains numerous historical and botanical exhibits pertaining to the Lajitas region.

While we were in the vicinity, I showed Cathy and our two sons where a mostly forgotten dirt airstrip had been located. Situated just to the west of the present-day center, the strip's original purpose was for use by the US Army Air Service during the Mexican Revolution. A generation of pioneering young aviators, including a certain Lieutenant Jimmy Doolittle, would build their careers upon what they learned while flying border patrol over the Big Bend. I took my first airplane ride from here, and during the 1960s mule races were staged on the runway in celebration of the Fourth of July. Though now abandoned, pieces of the vanishing strip are still visible running parallel to the south side of the Lajitas highway.

We coursed over to the trailhead a short distance away and strapped on our hiking gear. My plan was simple: go as far as we could around the backside of Contrabando Mountain to see some of the sights, and do some reminiscing with my sons about their family ancestors, now long passed. It is important for a young man to know where he came from; such knowledge can serve as a useful back azimuth when charting one's path into the future. Knowing how those who came before faced their own daily challenges and persevered can be a comfort when sailing your own stormy seas.

As Cathy was with us there was no attempt to go too far, too fast, nor did we attempt any cross-country traveling to speak of. Since neither she nor our sons had much inkling of what lay ahead other than from my stories, this trip would only serve as a baseline for other, more physically demanding walkabouts to come. We began moving north at a leisurely pace, the stark landscape stirring my memories as well as our senses as we walked along.

One of those memories pertained to the road itself: this was not the first track carved out of the desert headed for Camp Marfa. The original road began looping around Lajitas Mesa about a half mile west from the present trailhead, much nearer to the river. This older route skirted the very edge of the uplift, angling around until it intersected the new roadbed nearly a mile away to the north. Furthermore, this was not the only stretch where the present-day roadway strays from the original route in substantial fashion.

These lower strands of the Military Road run between the mesa and the westernmost branch of Comanche Creek, where in spots it is no further away than a fair shot with a short-barreled pistol. At about another mile beyond the aforementioned intersection, a large watering hole is located where the road crowds closest to this tributary. Though some say it is a spring and others claim it is a tinaja, the hole is actually both, which makes for a very reliable source; one of the very few near the route before it enters Fresno Creek. Approaching this landmark brought back another childhood memory, albeit an ugly one of murderous circumstance.

Recently I read about a brutal killing that occurred just outside of Terlingua. The perpetrator was being charged with murder, and the author of the article opined it was the first time anyone could recall such an appalling crime around here. I don't know who the writer interviewed in regard to that statement or if he made that little "fact" up on the fly, but the truth is there have been many murders in the lower Big Bend area throughout the years. One of the most haunting occurred about a mile east of this waterhole, and like so many of the others has remained unsolved to this day.

The newspapers of that time referred to the case as "The Lady in Chartreuse," and it started at the trading post on one of those blisteringly hot days in late July of 1965. Two of the locals who worked for my grandfather, Chon and Ramon Armendariz, rode in and told him of stumbling across a dead body on a hillside about three and a half miles northeast of Lajitas. The two men were a bit shaken by what they had seen at the site. Not certain of what might actually be out there, my grandfather saddled up a horse and headed cross-country to investigate.

What he found was a grisly sight that could have come from the pages of a Stephen King paperback. The mostly skeletal remains of a young woman were present, her body parts scattered about a crime scene that measured a couple of hundred feet in diameter. Evidently she had been dead for at least a month; wild animals had ripped apart her corpse and scattered what they hadn't eaten or carried completely off. Adding to a sense of the macabre was that she had been set on fire in an apparent attempt to destroy any forensic evidence. The remnants of her tattered and burned clothing were mostly chartreuse in color, thus supplying the headline for the case.

This horrific find was sensational enough to be picked up by the national news wires, and even the *New York Times* published an article concerning the gruesome crime. Sheriff Williams and Texas Ranger Arthur Hill were the investigating officers, and both men spent years trying to unravel what had actually occurred. Each man had his strong suspicions, but nothing concrete enough to ever properly serve justice.

Perhaps even more tragic than not being able to identify the killer was the fact that the two veteran peace officers were never even able to identify the victim. Her remains were ultimately

Contrabando Canyon

buried in a lonely grave on the east side of Austin, on paupers' grounds set aside for the anonymous dead who have no name and no one to mourn them. Over fifty years later, the circumstances surrounding her death remain a grim mystery.

Leaving the waterhole we continued north, taking note of the several deteriorating tracks and paths that wander out westerly toward Lajitas Mesa and Contrabando Mountain. These disappearing wisps of days gone by still serve as avenues into those rugged uplifts, as do the steepening arroyos that feed from both points of high ground into this fork of Comanche Creek. Others wander to places that are no longer there, save for some last decaying mementos once fashioned by man's hand and for his own purpose. The passage of time has now rendered these dead end spurs pointless.

However, one of these is yet another slice of an earlier version of the road between Lajitas and Marfa. It angles off to the northwest, while the more recent track continues due north to intersect what was the original route between the Mariposa mines and Marfa. These days, this section of the Mariposa road is referred to as the North Lone Star Mine Road. That is, until it joins with the remnants of the Military Road and heads toward the Whit-Roy diggings and Wax Factory Laccolith. One has to know something of the history of this country to avoid being totally confused, and even with that you can find yourself scratching your head from time to time. Yet that is the way of the Big Bend: people come and people go like the ebb and flow of waves washing along a shore, scrubbing the beach clean. When the next big wave of humankind arrives, they usually have no idea of who or what was there before.

We moved along the newer portion to where it tees into the North Lone Star Mine Road. Since we were still on state park land we decided to parallel this track west, trying to stay to higher ground so as to get a better view of what lay around us. Our little expedition shadowed the North Lone Star in this fashion for over a mile, until it veered northwesterly and we cut across country to another mining road that runs just above Contrabando Waterhole and the McGuirk Ruins.

Most people who come through here tend to think this was the original Contrabando Road, snaking its way for a short distance along the shoulder of the canyon before turning toward the mouth of the Fresno. In actuality though, this particular track was for the mining efforts that took place around the Contrabando Dome, and was located slightly north of the earlier route. The dome contained cinnabar ore, and during the 1930s the area was excavated extensively, mostly through the efforts of two men: Homer Wilson and Harris S. Smith.

Those who have spent much time in Big Bend National Park might recognize that first name, as this was the same Homer Wilson who had the ranch in Blue Creek Canyon below the Chisos Mountains. Wilson, a World War I veteran, was also a mining and petroleum engineer. He and Harris Smith, who at that time owned what is still referred to as the Smith Place some seven miles up Fresno Canyon, formed a business partnership together.

The alliance was a fruitful one, resulting in the creation of the Contrabando Dome and Fresno Mine companies as well as the establishment of a small nearby community known as *Buena Suerte*, which is Spanish for good luck. Now nothing more than a few disintegrating foundations along Fresno Creek, Buena Suerte sat along the Military Road where it drops into the canyon, opposite Wax Factory Laccolith. All of these operations shut down around the end of World War II, when cinnabar ore took another plunge in value.

From the point above Contrabando Waterhole and the Mc-

McGuirk Ruins

Guirk ruins, we left the mining track and descended into the canyon below. There is history in this small patch of desert foliage and bare rock nestled in the bottom of the crevice, as it encircles an invaluably reliable water source. It also provides evidence of an earlier chapter in H. W. McGuirk's full life before he ventured into Lajitas, and gives further testimony to the legacy this man left in the Big Bend country.

As best can be determined, McGuirk first tried his hand at ranching in the upper parts of the Solitario Mountains, near the head of Fresno Canyon. Having arrived in the area around 1885, he soon constructed what might be the oldest man-made landmark to be found in The Solitario: some large earthen dikes situated to capture runoff from the seasonal rains. They are still known as McGuirk's Tanks.

Sometime in the late 1890s McGuirk moved his headquarters to Contrabando Canyon, building a fairly large ranch house directly above Contrabando Waterhole. Made mostly with the materials at hand, this sturdy home was built out of rock and contained several rooms, a fireplace, and wood-framed windows and doorways. Nearby were livestock pens also formed from native rock, as well as a small trap, along with a collection of outbuildings. Even today, one can appreciate the attention to detail and the back-breaking labor involved in creating this place.

It was an excellent choice for a location, perhaps too much so for the comfort of some nameless others. The headquarters not only overlooked one of the best waterholes in the area, but it also acted as a chokepoint for anything moving either up or down that canyon. With a name like *contrabando*, which is Spanish for *contraband*, one can well imagine the consternation some might have felt at this strategic emplacement. Within two years McGuirk was forced to leave when the waterhole went bad. There was no logical reason for it to do so, and rumors persisted it had been poisoned.

Yet much like the land he had decided to settle upon, H. W. McGuirk was of a resilient nature. He secured a job with the Marfa-Mariposa Mining Company to maintain their telephone line, which ran through the eastern reaches of The Solitario, an area he was already intimately familiar with from prior experience. In doing so, he helped add to another bit of Big Bend history which has been mostly forgotten in recent years: the creation of the Telephone Trail.

With then-presiding Presidio County Judge H. H. Kilpatrick as his business partner, McGuirk went on to help form the Terlingua Mining Company. The decision to do so proved profitable; he completed his move to Lajitas and became that community's leading citizen until pulling up stakes in 1917. To my knowledge H.W. McGuirk never returned to the Big Bend after that. A few years later, he passed away in Deming, New Mexico, at the age of seventy-one.

My family and I wandered through these ruins, taking in the remnants of a dream by someone who had vision coupled with the work ethic needed to make his dream a reality. Much of the walls of the home still remain intact, though the roof and portal frames are long gone. Nevertheless, the care put into its construction is plainly evident, as is that reflected in the rock pens some three hundred yards up canyon. I have never heard of anyone who tried to live here after McGuirk abandoned this place, but his handiwork has managed to remain standing against the encroaching Chihuahuan Desert for more than a century. A man should leave his mark someplace, and Howard Washington McGuirk certainly left his here.

On the Old Military Road heading for the Fresno

Before leaving we were able to more closely examine what remains of the original Contrabando Road, which ran through the middle of the McGuirk headquarters. This wagon track stayed largely within the canyon itself, following the gorge past the ruins until it cut across some higher ground and then moved on to what we used to call Fresno Farm, located where Fresno Creek empties into the Rio Grande. A turnoff to the farm was part of this route, winding its way around the main house located there and then on to the river itself. These days the lower part of the road is generally easier to locate than the upper portion, as the sections that most closely followed the canyon have been washed away.

With our curiosity concerning the ruins satisfied, we decided to work our way up the canyon and scout for more sign of Contrabando Road, or what was left of it. The track is plainly visible until you get past the rock pens, and then it disappears into the creek bottom, only to show itself again another two hundred yards or so upstream. These bits and pieces continue up the canyon until the wagon trail tees into Military Road.

My grandparents: Edward Benton "Ben" English and wife Angie

From the ruins we began drifting back toward Lajitas and the trailhead across from the Warnock Center. There were still some daylight hours left, and sufficient time to revisit some more of my memories along the way. In less than a quarter of a mile, we detoured to that earlier segment of the Lajitas-Marfa route mentioned earlier. This section stays closer to the shoulder of Contrabando Mountain and provides a slightly shorter trip back. But beyond that, it was the track my grandmother used all those years ago on our frequent trips to Fresno Canyon. Revisiting childhood memories is always a special thing, especially when they are really good ones.

As I walked the same ground I had covered nearly fifty years ago those recollections reached out to me, rushing through my mind like the flow of a high mountain stream after the first snowmelt. The familiar scenery provided ample kindling to feed long-dormant thoughts, and the intervening decades faded away to where being five years old seemed like just yesterday. My grandmother was a fine partner to have along on most any adventure; some might say it was because she was still a kid at heart herself who refused to grow up.

Yet that statement does an injustice to who she really was, as well as to her true essence and strength. With my grandmother it was much more a case of never really growing old, and there is a huge difference between the two. After all, it was she who taught me to spin a top and shoot marbles, and she made for the best shortstop I ever had in a game of baseball. There was a special spark within her that glowed every single day of her life.

As the shadows lengthened to intertwine with the coming of evening, there were also many thoughts of my grandfather. Throughout the intervening decades I have found it impossible to think of one without recollecting about the other. They were married when they were quite young, and like the Good Book says, "The two shall become one." As their time together spread out before them and life's trail behind became longer, those two certainly did. He had a deep, quiet, abiding love for this land that was never much spoken about in word but far more richly illustrated in action and in deed. Papa was that way about all the things that he cherished most.

Perhaps in some small way I have given voice in these chapters to what he himself felt. In growing older this has become more important to me, more urgent: providing a way to communicate for those who can no longer speak about the Big Bend and what it meant to them. Their long silence is not an indication of lack of commitment or emotion. It is only because they and their kind were too busy *doing* to spend much time expressing themselves in mere words.

Consequently this is how the history of this country has become so confused and convoluted: men came with their hopes and dreams, had their defeats and their victories, and then moved on or died. In essence, they were too involved in their struggle to carve out a life in this singular land to write or say much about it. It was their way, and the way of the desert they loved so much. In a present time when narcissism and self-aggrandizement seem an epidemic among those who have actually done so little, there is much to be admired in the ways of those who did so much in an unpresuming manner.

As for me, I find an indescribable yearning growing within my heart, a childlike longing to work cattle alongside my grandfather just one more time in the Fresno, or ease along the old Military Road with my grandmother in that Scout; two yahoos headed for the far country with one eye on the road and the other peeled for some free venison along the way.

EPILOGUE

For each morning with its light,
For rest and shelter of the night:
For health and food for love and friends,
For everything Thy Goodness brings.

—RALPH WALDO EMERSON

There are certain places in this world that seize the soul of those who journey into their environs. They tantalize our senses, both physical and otherwise, with a thousand varieties of awe, wonderment, mystery, and exultation. Even though we may only visit them but once, the mental snapshots we develop during the event never seem to fade or go away, remaining firmly entrenched within our psyches from that moment forward until death's bed or beyond. Someone once said that life is not a series of years, but a recollection of special moments. The same can be said about those special places exemplified by the Big Bend of Texas.

These same moments and places call for a more introspective look at ourselves and where we fit into the larger scheme of things, which often enough leads us to questions about those who came before. Did they truly see and appreciate what was here, or were they so involved in their existential struggles as to not take much notice of the rare natural beauty surrounding them? What did they learn from this unique land, what enigmas did they unravel here? For many, we will never know, as their stories have been irretrievably lost, trapped in a void of forgotten memories or anonymity. They were too busy living history to have the opportunity or inclination to leave written documents of it. Their implacable enemy was time, or to be more accurate, the lack thereof.

As I have grown older the true value of time has become more apparent to me, and far more precious. It is the one thing we cannot change, call back, speed up, or slow down. With all of our advanced technological marvels and attending vanities, time pays no more attention to our needs and schemes than we of a tiny fleck of dust lying upon parched, barren soil. Time remains the unchanging constant in our mortal continuance, concerned with nothing else but its unrelenting march forward.

Yet this does not mean we mere mortals don't entertain fanciful wishes of being able to bend it to our petty wills. As the decades have passed by, I have found myself wishing that I had just one hour to talk with Aunt Mag about the Hot Springs, "Sis" Hay concerning early Marfa, or Grandfather Cash regarding his days as an underaged infantryman in Lajitas. Much more so, I wish I had just one more hour to sit with my father and Papa English and hear their voices again. The two of them prowled a big part of this region of the Big Bend, spurred on by a consuming passion for this land and what there was to be learned from it.

In the furtherance of their quest each made a habit of seeking out *los viejos,* the old ones who had been there since the time of the first mining boom at the foot of California Mountain. Most of these *viejos* were of Mexican heritage, as very few early Anglos ever lived their entire lives in the lower reaches of the Big Bend. Usually they pushed on for someplace else once they had enriched themselves in some way, went bust, or completed whatever tasks had put them there.

But the Mexican families stayed on, often with generation following generation. They did not live on the land for just a little while; rather they became part and parcel of their surroundings, acquiring a thorough education in its many secrets and peculiarities as one era led to the next. Unfortunately, most were so busy surviving their harsh conditions there was precious little time to write of what they had learned, even on the off-chance they might had been literate enough to do so. What did manage to be passed on was usually done verbally, and in their native tongue, as few spoke any kind of English. When these men died, much of their hard-won knowledge died along with them.

My father and grandfather spoke fluent Spanish and sought out those stories to expand their own trove of knowledge. They acted as amateur historians in this respect, but unfortunately also neglected to write down what had been revealed to them. After they passed away all I was left with were some old maps, fading photographs, and my childhood recollections. It is a regrettable loss; they were intelligent, well-read men with a natural curiosity for this country and those who had been here before them.

This loss is felt even more acutely when you consider that for all practical purposes, the late 1950s through the late 1960s were somewhat of a lost decade for this area. There was only the smallest handful of people living here during that period, and most who did seemed to be present one day and gone the next. The mines were by and large shut down, which led to a big drop in population from where it had stood in the 1940s or even most of the 1950s. The lower parts of Brewster and adjoining swaths of Presidio County weren't just a couple of old ghost towns and abandoned sites scattered hither and yon; in the early 1960s this faraway, isolated stretch of border country was more like a *tierra de las fantasmas,* if one cared to calculate on such a scale.

It was well before cell phones or hardly any other kind of telephone service, and electricity of any sort was a true luxury. Outdoor toilets were still the norm, as many homes did not have modern plumbing. Television was something that people in far off places enjoyed, and even AM radio was only able to entertain during the nighttime hours, unless you favored the occasional high-wattage station beaming out of northern Mexico. The Big Bend was so remote that few ventured into its domains for the purpose of relaxation; a bona fide tourist was not a common sight and usually could be better categorized as an amateur rock hound or aspiring geologist. By and large the region was only miles upon miles of lonesomeness, which is just the way most of the inhabitants liked it.

The double-edged broadsword of technology began to change all this in the 1970s. It brought a new and completely different era to the region; some of it for the better and some for the worse. The Big Bend I knew as a kid is mostly dead and gone now, at least the parts that people have tried to "improve" upon. I suppose a person from the 1920s would have the same thought about the 1960s Big Bend I grew up in, and someone from the 1880s would feel the same about the 1920s. Such is how change and human nature conspire to divide the generations.

Currently some of this territory resembles a version of the nightmarish junkyard planet portrayed in the science-fiction film *Soldier.* Given enough time, the desert will reclaim its own, and the resulting scars will start to fade away. Even so, some of these contemporary eyesores will in turn become sunburned, rotted, and destitute enough to attract the curiosity of those who come later upon the scene. Just as we eagerly set out to find the relics and residue of those who came before us, so will others be intrigued by what we leave behind in the present. It has been said many times that one man's trash is another man's treasure; the same holds true from one epoch to the next.

No measure can be taken of any land without speaking of those who make use of it. What they hold to be true and inviolate sets the tone for what will happen to that ground in the future. In this respect there are basically two competing groups and philosophies, championed by those who think upon themselves as land owners versus those who consider themselves more as people of the land. The latter have a deep emotional attachment to what they stand upon and desire to keep it as naturally pristine as possible. The former faction sees whatever land within their grasp mostly in terms of how much wealth can be extracted from it; the long-term results are of secondary importance.

Though some may find this perspective to be overly simplistic or demeaning to one group or the other, it nevertheless cuts straight to the heart of the matter. The Big Bend country of Texas has had ample quantities of both breeds, as well as ample evidence of where strict adherence to each of the two philosophies can lead. In reality our nation needs both groups to successfully meet the unending challenges we face as a society, but there should be certain locales set aside that deserve the respect and the support of both parties for the mutual benefit of all.

President Theodore Roosevelt understood these competing philosophies and the irreversible effects they can bring about. Of his lifetime of many grand achievements, the concept of a national park system was one of his finest. He and the many others who shared this admirable goal helped make a reality of such invaluable contributions as the Big Bend National Park. Equally important in this has been the dedication and hard work of state officials and conservationists that gave the citizens of Texas a state park system to be proud of. In this the Big Bend is doubly blessed; it is home to not only an exquisite *national* park but also one of the largest and most charismatic *state* parks to be found anywhere in the United States.

Yet the foundational element in this, and far more essential than any level of government, is the individual citizen. The Big Bend has been repeatedly lauded by many of our fellows who profoundly care about this land and intuitively comprehend just how special it really is. They understand that God did not give us such splendor to have it defiled and abused, as so many other areas in our part of Texas have been. We as a people should never take this priceless gift lightly and need to pay proper homage to those with the forbearance to see what was being lost, and the personal courage to go forth and do what needed done to halt the ensuing blight.

For myself I will enjoy the Big Bend as long as possible in the most intimate way one can, on my own two feet—sometimes going where no trail has ever been known to run. Early on I made a promise to myself not only to go and see, but to write about what I learned and experienced. This book contains only a few of the hundreds of stories I could tell about this country, and before I die I hope for many more to come. There are still so many unseen places and things in this land to take note of. You see, unlike my ancestors, I plan to leave many a journal about my travels and what I happen to discover along the way. This country keeps you humble; it seems the more I find out, the less I think I actually knew and the more unanswered questions I am left with.

An intricate part of this process has been my wife Cathy, who refers to the Big Bend as my "one and only mistress." She should know, as she is the one who has listened to my stories since we first met over thirty years ago. It was where we honeymooned, and on every single opportunity offered from that point forward, we went back. When our sons were old enough to have an opinion about a family outing, their first pick was almost always the Big Bend. After they grew up and started their own lives, it was Cathy who encouraged me to take those many solitary sabbaticals there for four or five days at a time. And it was she who was my biggest encouragement in writing the lines you are reading now.

Recently the Big Bend has become even more central to our lives. After nearly thirty years of living in Ozona, Cathy and I have finally made the dream of moving back a reality. With the encouragement of our sons and a lot of prayer to a benevolent God, we have found a place in Alpine that was made to order for us. As I write this, we are still in the process of completing the move and thrilled with what we see in our near future. It's been a

The Rancherias Trail, Big Bend State Park

long time coming, but perhaps that is why the reality seems even sweeter than any of our dreams. Somehow I am also certain my family ancestors mentioned in this book would heartily approve of this particular development. It's just something in the genes, I suppose.

Our new home will also allow others who share our passion to come and visit. Starting when our sons were attending Annapolis, they began bringing home fellow servicemen, and together we would introduce them to what the early Spanish explorers referred to as *El Desplobado*. Each of those trips holds special memories, as they allowed me to get to know some of the finest men I've shared a campfire with. If you ever despair in thinking all is lost for our nation's collective tomorrows, I suggest you spend some quality time with this remarkable breed of young Americans. It'll cure your pessimism in record time.

These trips became popular enough at Annapolis to be given a name by our guests: "Mr. English's Afghanistan Training." I wouldn't say that Cathy cooked and cleaned and entertained for an army during those years, but she certainly cooked and cleaned and entertained for many a veteran or promising young officer of the Marine Corps or Navy. It seemed we usually had more wanting to come than we had room to take aboard, and once they experienced the Big Bend, they invariably wanted to venture back.

Enough time has passed now that some of our former guests have in turn shown others what is so extraordinary about this country. Passing along such a worthy tradition is something that we as a family have found very rewarding. Once settled in our new home, it will give us plenty of opportunity to continue to do so in the future.

When I am gone it is my sincerest wish that my sons and their sons not yet born will be able to keep this pattern going for generations to come. What lies in the Big Bend has been scarred and disfigured by man's hand on occasion, but perhaps therein lies the enduring mystique in its totality. It is an old and enduring story that is still being played out. For man to struggle against nature in one manner or another is as deeply ingrained in our being as the need to breathe or reproduce. This basic drive has taken us across the seas, marched us across the continents, plunged us to the greatest depths, and placed us upon the highest mountaintops. It has taken us to the moon, and someday shall carry us to unknown planets and worlds now only depicted in the pages of science fiction. It is a big world out there, but our universe is immeasurably larger.

And through it all there is one thing of which I am certain: this land that I choose to call home will remain and shall triumph in the end.

Ben H. English
Alpine, Texas

Until we meet again, may the
Good Lord take a liking to you.

—ROY ROGERS

ABOUT THE AUTHOR

An eighth-generation Texan, Ben H. English was raised mostly in the Lajitas-Terlingua area. An honors graduate of Angelo State University, he served in the United States Marine Corps for seven years, was a high school teacher, and retired after twenty-two years in the Texas Highway Patrol.